HAYES, HARI and CRANFORD during WORLD WAR ONE 1914-1918

Tanya Britton

© Tanya Britton 2001-2010

All rights reserved. No part of this publication may be reproduced, stored in a retrieval system, or transmitted in any form or by any means, electronic, mechanical or otherwise, without prior permission of the copyright holder.

ISBN
978-0-9927922-1-3

ACKNOWLEDGEMENTS

Uxbridge Local History Library, Cathy Kelter, Philip Sherwood, Terry White, Mr. and Mrs Broughton, Eric Button, Stephen Britton, Douglas and Eileen Rust, the late Fred Badcock, Joss Martin and Ken Pearce

CONTENTS
Introduction

Setting the scene	1
War is declared	18
Recruitment	21
Employment	28
Leisure Pursuits	63
Transport	66
Rationing and the Cultivation of Land Order	76
Fund Raising and Relief	88
Defence	94
Police	102
Boy Scouts and Girl Guides	106
Air-Raids	109
Refugees and Evacuees	117
Housing	119
Schools	125
Health	132
Hospitals	140
Prisoners of War	146
Alien internees and Spy Fever	149
Armistice	153
War Memorials	157

INTRODUCTION

Hayes, Harlington and Cranford are all ancient villages and all are in the Hundred of Elthorne. Originally five separate villages formed the area now known as Hayes – Hayes Town, Wood End, Botwell, Yeading and Hayes End. Harlington, which lies to the south of Hayes and borders on to it, was anciently called Herdington, Herdyngton or Hardyngton. Cranford, on the eastern side of the River Crane, is an Anglo-Saxon name.

Both Harlington and Cranford lie on the Bath Road – an old stagecoach route from London to Bath. In Harlington parish churchyard stood a famous old yew tree, hundreds of years old. At one time two yew trees stood in the churchyard.

In 1665 many people fled from London to Hayes and Harington to escape the plague. Several were clubbed to death by villagers, fearful of themselves becoming infected. On the northern boundary of Harlington the 'Dawley Wall' was constructed in the late 18th century, it is said, to keep out the smallpox or the plague.

During the latter half of the 19th century industrialization began and by 1914 the villages were becoming almost unrecognizable and by the eve of war had sufficiently developed to allow them to play an important part in the daily struggles which any war can bring.

My thanks are extended to the Local History Library staff at Uxbridge Library for their co-operation, Philip Sherwood, Cathy Kelter, Hayes History Society, Stephen Britton and Eric Button.

SETTING THE SCENE

The period between 1902 when the Boer War had ended and the beginning of the Great War in August 1914 was one of peace and comparative economic stability, but not advance, although the period was a time of war scares. July was the time for holidays, this year the most brilliant summer for years, and August the time of annual training. The Territorial Army, and many of its units were already mustered in camp whilst others were about to go into camp that weekend. The local 'E' Company, 8th Middlesex V.B. Regiment was on the outbreak of war at Salisbury Plain for its annual training. It had been there since July.

Wood End Green, Hayes. (Hillingdon Local Studies, Archives and Museum Service)

At the time of the First World War, Hayes, Harlington and Cranford were quite separate parishes, each with its own church, and after the war ended, each had its own war memorial. Hayes and Harlington amalgamated in 1930. Hayes Workhouse had been constructed in 1803 at the corner of Golden Crescent and Printing House Lane, which at one time was called Workhouse Lane. It closed when Hayes became part of the Uxbridge Union. The dreaded workhouse at Hillingdon, which had opened in 1747 was enlarged in 1838 to become the workhouse for Cowley, Hayes, Hillingdon and Uxbridge, West Drayton, Ruislip, Ickenham and Harefield. At one period in 1911 there had been as many as 282 unfortunate inmates, although for the following years the numbers tended to be less. In 1930 it became part of Hillingdon Hospital. Staines Board of Guardians covered the areas of Harlington, Harmondsworth and Cranford. The workhouse was situated in Ashford and later became part of Ashford Hospital.

The Queen's Head, Cranford
(Hillingdon Local Studies, Archives and Museum Service)

St. Mary's Church in Church Road has a 13th century chancel. The Church is approached by a 16th century lych gate. The north aisle is of 15th century construction as is the west tower. The south aisle dates from the early 16th century. A brass marking the grave of Robert Leslie who died in about 1370 is reputed to be the oldest in Middlesex. He had been one of the rectors there. There was a Wesleyan Methodist Chapel, Morgans Lane Tabernacle, which was in operation by 1895. John Wesley and George Whitefield preached at Hayes in the 18th century and as a result Hayes Town Chapel had been formed.

In 1910 a district chapelry was established at Botwell in Golden Crescent. Four years later a new mission church was built on the corner of Nield Road and Station Road, which was replaced in 1929 on the same site by St. Anselms. At Yeading a mission church had been established by 1890. It was formerly a day school.

As a direct result of the Grand Union Canal, which opened in 1794, the brickfields around Hayes and West Drayton grew and became the most important industry in the area. Many docks had been built alongside the canal at Hayes during the 19th and early 20th centuries but by 1864 most of these brickfields had been worked out, although some at Yeading and near Hayes Bridge continued in use until the 20th century. The agrarian environment in Yeading had changed little until the 19th century when the Grand Union Canal was extended and by the time of the outbreak of war was still a tiny hamlet. Hayes UDC was planning to purchase the Council office and site for working class dwellings at Yeading as part of the Housing Scheme and to replace White's Row, a group of cottages, which were considered a health hazard. Manor Farm, the history of which can be dated back to 1307, was the most important farm in Yeading with 180 acres of land with outbuildings and tied cottages. It was rented by Mr. E. Liddall, a councillor from 1904. Corn and hay for the London markets were grown. By 1902 there was a Smallpox isolation hospital here which was situated roughly midway between the Ruislip Road and Willow Tree Lane. The Pound for stray animals was still in existence, situated near the Cage (a short stay prison for minor offences) which once stood on Church Green. The Pound at Harlington also once stood close to the Cage in the centre of the village.

Apart from brickbuilding there were few industries in Hayes in the late 19th century. By 1874, a large proportion of the residents lived at Hayes End, Wood End, Botwell and Yeading, rather than at Hayes. Hayes Cottage Hospital had opened on Grange Road towards the end of the 19th century when Hayes was still a small village. It treated 20 to 25 patients annually. The hospital replaced an earlier one which had been built in Freemans Lane.

More scope for local development occurred with the opening of the Great Western Railway line from Paddington to Reading in 1840. West Drayton then became the first stop out of London, allowing greater movement of labour and goods to and from the capital. The line opened to Bristol in 1841. The GWR laid down a telegraph from Paddington to West Drayton but made no use of it for its own purpose and it was removed in 1849. In 1850 the GWR had a change of heart and introduced it all over their system. Hayes and Harlington Station had been opened in 1864 on the line. Widening powers had been obtained from Parliament in 1873 which went as far as West Drayton. On August 16th 1876 the line from West Drayton to Southall was opened up. Two additional lines were lengthened from Southall to West Drayton on November 25th 1878 and extended to the east end of Maidenhead Bridge by September 18th 1874. On August 12th 1878 the lines were used between Hayes and West Drayton. There was also a line running to

Brentford which was used for goods traffic as well as for passengers.

On 12th May 1870 the Southall, Ealing and Shepherds Bush TramRailway was incorporated. In 1872, before the construction began, its engineer, George Billington, promoted an extension from Southall to Uxbridge, which was unsuccessful. A Light Railway Order was sought for an extension along the Uxbridge Road to Southall, Hayes and Uxbridge. Uxbridge, Hillingdon, Southall and Hayes were all in favour. Uxbridge was particularly enthusiastic being served only by the GWR. A petition was drawn up at the beginning of 1898 which drew 6,000 signatures in favour. The Council adopted the resolution and sent it to the LUT. The Order, which was ultimately rejected, was made on 9th May 1899. Work began on London United Tramways route from Southall to Uxbridge on July 27th 1903. The opening of the route was delayed as the depot and the electricity substation at Hillingdon Heath had not been built. The substation could, if necessary, be fed from the substation at Hounslow. The first daily tram arrived at the end of May 1904 on the route Shepherds Bush to Southall and Uxbridge via Acton. Some days later on 5th June 1904 another new service came into operation from Shepherds Bush to Uxbridge on Sundays only. By 1904 there was also a daily service from Hammersmith to Uxbridge via Hanwell and Southall and another service from Hammersmith through Brentford and Southall to Uxbridge. By the time of the outbreak of war, most of the tracks (mostly a single line with loops) had been renewed. As from 5th June 1904 there was a Sunday service in operation between Shepherds Bush and Uxbridge. By the year 1907 there was also a daily service from

Hammersmith to Uxbridge via Brentford and Southall.

In 1899 The Hayes Development Company acquired land south of the hamlet of Botwell, at that time the industrial hub of the town, and started to attract industry to the area. At the start of the war there were roughly 1,100 houses in the Hayes district and the population stood at roughly 4,700.

A LUET tram on the Shepherd's Bush to Uxbridge route, early 20th Century (Hillingdon Local Studies, Archives and Museum Service)

A housing scheme for Botwell with 208 houses had been agreed and plans were afoot to start building. In 1900 the first business, J.A. King and Company, which specialised in making fireproof partitions, began manufacturing. The first large factory was the British Electric Transformer Company, makers of electrical equipment, which arrived at Clayton Road in 1901, followed by Arthur Lee and Brothers, a marble-making, slate and granite works, in 1902 on the site of a former laundry. In 1904 some sidings on the GWR were constructed by the Hayes Development Company, serving all parts of the estate, which were later extended. The town in the years prior to war had seen a growth in the industries coming to the area, the workers coming from anywhere between Paddington and Windsor. Good road and rail services and the

Grand Union Canal together with low rents and rates were prominent factors, which induced firms to settle at Hayes. Musical instruments, preserves and other food products were the most important manufacturers, the latter because of the local fruit-growing industry Some old dilapidated buildings had been demolished and Hayes Council had started housing projects with the building of Rosedale Avenue in 1912 but by 1913 there was further increasing demand for cottages and houses, particularly in the industrial district around Hayes Station. House building could not keep up with industrial development and with the influx of so many workers there was a chronic shortage of housing.

Calf Provision Merchant (Hillingdon Local Studies, Archives and Museum Service)

By 1912 there had been a growing awareness of the problems created since 1851 by London's rapid expansion. The population of Harlington in 1901 was 1,690, and at Hayes in 1901 it was 2,594 but had grown to 4,261 by 1911. The 1911 census showed that one-tenth of the population of England was living in overcrowded conditions and it was estimated that between 5 and 10% of urban workmen were living in slums. The population of Hayes had increased from 1901 to 1911 by 64.3% and by 1913 had risen to approximately 4,750. By the time war broke out, the population of the Urban District of Hayes was not far short of 20,000. The new Housing Act of 1909 vested powers in Local Authorities to, should they wish, prepare town-planning schemes.

The Hayes Advisory Housing and Town Planning Committee approached the Local Government Board and had requested a public enquiry, which reported in June 1913. To this end, 50 cottages were built at Wood End and in March 1914 the Council acquired over 14 acres to be developed on 'garden suburb lines'. At Botwell, Hayes UDC was negotiating with Mr. J. Odell for the surrender of Glebe Field with a view to developing the estate. Plans had been approved and an application was made to the Local Government Board for sanction to raise a loan. Once this had been received the Council proposed to proceed to erect 52 houses fronting Station Road and Coldharbour Lane. Land had been acquired for the erection of 22 houses at Yeading and the Council had also bought about 14 acres of land at Botwell to build 208 houses.

By 1911 there were 15 major companies and the brick-making industry had declined considerably, although Hayes was predominately an agricultural area at that time. In Silverdale Road, the Orchestrelle Company opened in 1909 with further extensions in 1912. They also had a factory in Germany. A central block was used by the Universal Music Company for producing music rolls for pianolas – mechanical pianos. Their head office was situated at Aeolian Hall, New Bond Street in London. This was followed by the X-Chair Patents Co. Ltd., specialising in folding tables and chairs, which had moved to Hayes from Clerkenwell and in 1913-14 came Scott's Preserves Limited.

In 1911 Harrison's and Sons Printing Office, printers of stamps (it had at that time the complete Government contract for making all British and some foreign stamps for other Government departments), pension books, government papers etc., settled at Hayes on land acquired on the north side of the canal, which became known as Printing House Lane, as did the Goss Printing Press Company of Chicago on land between Blyth Road and the railway. Valentine Ord and Company, manufacturers of saccharine and glucose etc also moved here as well as other companies, the most important of which was The Gramophone Company (HMV), which had moved its HQ from London to Hayes where it backed onto the Great Western Railway main line with a siding into the factory. It was situated on 11 acres. The foundation stone of the company, which was planning gramophone manufacture, was laid by Dame Nellie Melba in 1907. By the time of the start of the war well over 1,000 and possibly as many as 3,000 people came to work at Hayes by train or by tram every morning. Some distance away near Hayes End, the Beck Engineering Company Limited set up its registered office at Eden Works on the Uxbridge Road behind the Adam and Eve pub, opposite the entrance to Church Road, in May 1912. The company was a tool makers and iron foundry.

Although the suburban expansion of London in the nineteenth century was great and high rents were forcing workers to move to cheaper areas and commute, in some instances the population had doubled in the space of seven years, the London Borough of Hillingdon was still largely unaffected by this spread. At the turn of the 20th century, Uxbridge was the only town of any size, although Ruislip, Hayes, West Drayton and Harlington had small centres of population.

In 1901 a reformatory for young Jewish boys, later known as the Hayes Industrial School for Jewish Boys, had opened, thanks to the generosity of the. Rothschild family of Acton and elsewhere. Its only headmaster until it closed in about 1937 was Mr. Israel Ellis. It was situated on the corner of Uxbridge Road and Coldharbour Lane and pioneered the humane treatment of young male offenders. The boys, who came from all over the country, were all Jewish but the same was not true for most if not all of the masters. Here arable land was cultivated by the boys, especially those wishing to emigrate to Canada under the Salvation Army scheme. There were three Public Elementary School in the Hayes district at that time – Hayes Council School in Clayton Road (Clayton Road School), Dr. Triplett's School, situated in Hayes Town (which was badly in need of additional class room to accommodate the increasing population) and Yeading Elementary School. A church infant school was opened at Dawley in 1897. The Elisha Biscoe School in Tentelow Lane at Norwood served the educational needs of the poor of Hayes, although most went to the National School at Wood End Green after it was built.

Dr. Triplett's School was formerly the Hayes National Infant School which had opened in 1836. Thomas Triplett had taught at Hayes and when he died in July 1670 he was buried in Westminster Abbey (Poet's Corner). He had estates in Suffolk and one of his bequests was to provide £15 annually to apprentice children in the Parish of Hayes. Three eighths of the income of Dr. Triplett's charity was allocated to Dr. Triplett's School. There had also been a small schoolhouse at Orchard Cottage in Freemans Lane. In 1884 it was converted to a house. It was here that James Gibbons was murdered by his wife in that same year. The house is now demolished.

Harlington in ancient records is called Herdington, Herdyngton or Hardyngton – the modern name dates from about the 1700s. A Roman camp was discovered when Heathrow Airport was constructed at the boundary of Heathrow and Harlington. It is believed to have been Caesar's camp after he crossed the Thames. William Byrd, who is recognised as being one of the greatest of the Tudor composers, lived at Harlington from 1577 until 1593. He was a firm Catholic and was often prosecuted as a recusant. The parish church is dedicated to the Saints Peter and Paul and is an ancient structure, originally constructed in the 12th century At some time the churchyard contained two ancient yew trees. Until 1825 the periodical clipping of the trees into artificial shapes was a village holiday. The original Baptist Chapel was erected at the end of the 18th century. In 1857, the population was under 1,000 and by the turn of the 20th century, Harlington was still mainly farmland, market gardens growing fresh vegetables for the London market, and brickfields. The Parish lies on an old stagecoach route from London to Bath, as does Cranford, notorious in the days of highwaymen, who preyed on vulnerable travellers as they made their way across the vast wastes of Hounslow Heath. Dawley Wall, which lies on the northern boundary of the Parish is one miles in length and was reputedly constructed to keep out smallpox. It was the park wall of the former Dawley estate and was built in the late 18th century. A National School was opened in 1848 jointly by Harlington and Cranford Parish Councils but situated in Harlington. Schoolchildren from both villages attended the school until a national School was opened in Cranford in 1883 when the younger children transferred. The nearest station was Hayes and Harlington, on the Great Western Railway.

The centre of the village of Harlington c1910, showing the Baptist Church (Hillingdon Local Studies, Archives and Museum Service)

The Parish of Cranford is bounded by Hayes and Norwood on the north, Heston on the east, Harlington on the west and on the south by Bedfont. It is an ancient Parish and was mentioned in the survey of Domesday. It is in the Hundred of Elthorne and is now mostly in the London Borough of Hounslow, but parts, including Cranford Park and St. Dunstan's Church, are situated in the London Borough of Hillingdon. The village, a mile away from the church, also lies on the road to Bath. The name Cranford is derived from the ford over the small river Crane. The ancient parish church, dedicated to St. Dunstan, is a small building which accommodates a congregation of only 90 people. The tower and chancel date from about the 15th century, although the top storey is brick-built, having been rebuilt in 1716. However, time does not stand still.

Although the suburban expansion of London and high rents were forcing workers to move to cheaper areas and commute, Cranford was unaffected by this spread. In 1801 there were 27 houses and after the enclosure in 1820 the village began to grow slowly, increasing to 117 houses in 1901. In the later 19th century, market-gardening commenced in the Parish on a large scale. In 1899 there was much fruit grown in the parish, with strawberries and other soft fruits grown under apple and pear trees. One grower in the parish had 45 acres of fruit and flowers, including 7 acres of strawberries and at some time there were two others, with respectively 20 acres and 30 acres of flower. At this date it was said that 'The price and rent of land in the parish, which is quite out of the route of suburban dwellings, are unaccountably high, and labour is dear'. By the late 1880s, the population had risen to around 1,600 people. Cranford was host to one of the few local Druid circles which existed at that time.

Harlington, Cranford and Harmondsworth Cottage Hospital (Hillingdon Local Studies, Archives and Museum Service)

A cottage hospital was situated in the Sipson Road and served Harlington, Harmondsworth and Cranford. Staines Board of Guardians covered the areas of Cranford, Harlington and Harmondsworth. The workhouse was in Ashford, and later became part of Ashford Hospital.

In 1848 a National school was opened jointly by Harlington and Cranford Parish Councils. By 1870 the average attendance had risen to nearly 120. There were also three small private elementary schools. When a National school was opened in Cranford in 1883 for girls and infants, the children from there, except at first for the older boys, were withdrawn from Harlington. The older boys continued to attend the Harlington School for some years, but were also accommodated at Cranford by 1899. By the end of the century the National School had about 160 pupils in attendance and the infant school about 25.

Between 1870 and 1901 elementary education had become firmly established and schools had been constructed in the first decade of the 20th century to meet the rising population. Some developments in elementary schools had taken place, including higher standards of teacher training and improved curricula with more emphasis on practical subjects. Secondary education was almost non-existent, although some private secondary schools did exist and Uxbridge County School, the first secondary school in the modern-day Borough, which later became Bishopshalt, opened in the Greenway on 11th September 1907 and was co-educational. By the outbreak of World War One there were six times as many children in secondary schools as in 1900, and there were increases in the numbers of scholarship winners. Many schools were in need of enlarging.

Back Lane and bridge, Cranford, in winter (Hillingdon Local Studies, Museum and Archive Service)

The Development of Roads and Funds Act of 1909 brought the Roads Board into existence and many conferences were held before and during 1914 by all the local authorities to consider the arterial roads question very carefully. The Middlesex County Council , almost on the eve of war, arranged to proceed immediately with the Great West Road, which was in urgent need of building. It was to be commenced at the Bath Road end of the proposed road and as money was not a problem, it was urged that the road should be commenced in order to absorb the unemployed.

The Council Offices and Hayes Cottage Hospital, early 20th century. (Hillingdon Local Studies, Archives and Museum Service)

The provision of social amenities to meet the expansion of population after 1890 proceeded slowly. The range of entertainment available to ordinary Londoners was not particularly extensive. In fact, there was not a great deal of leisure for most working people except on Saturday night and on Sundays. On weekdays they could read, play card games or have a sing-song around the piano. Silent films were well established before the War, and cinema was already popular. In Middlesex at the outbreak of 1914-18 War there were 80 cinemas licensed, but as yet there were no dance halls. The first purpose-built cinema in Hayes opened in 1913 in Station Road. The Licensing Committee allowed no Sunday films at this time. Other entertainments such as charity and variety concerts were also held in the cinemas.

Many sports clubs had started before the turn of the 20th century, amongst them were Staines and West Middlesex Golf Club which was inaugurated in 1890. Lansdowne Tennis Club, a badminton club and a cricket club were located in Harlington by 1913. In Hayes the Working Men's Institute and tennis, football clubs, including the Botwell Mission F.C. which was formed in 1909 and Hayes United F.C which was inaugurated before the commencement of hostilities Uxbridge and Hayes United Football Club's ground was at Rectory Farm. Cricket clubs were all in existence prior to 1895, the Hayes Cricket Club in about 1894. Harlington Football Club was in existence by 1908 and here there was also cricket club. Cycle clubs were at Hayes and Harlington. Several men from the Hayes area belonged to the St. George's Athletic and Social Club at Southall, which had in all just over 100 members.

Unemployment was a problem immediately prior to the war and there had been plenty of unemployment parades. Some local men had been lured to new lives in Canada, New Zealand or Australia. Agitation was mounting on behalf of womens' rights and the suffragette movement had local supporters. In mid 1914 suffragettes were threatening to destroy Harlington Church, parts of which date from the 12th century. It had to be constantly guarded for several weeks. The War intervened just in time to save the church from a disastrous fate.

The European situation was getting blacker, although the impasse of Home Rule for Ireland was predominant in people's minds. War clouds were looming..........

WAR IS DECLARED...

The declaration of War between Austria and Serbia on 29th July 1914 seemed sudden. All hopes of peace were gradually abandoned and on the morning of 4th August 1914 Britain declared war on Germany. The announcement was greeted with relief by many. The War would be over by Christmas, the 'Hun' taught a lesson and victory would be won. Patriotic fervour was the order of the day. Excitement abounded.

Banks closed their doors and crowds of panic-stricken people flocked to all the local shops to buy food and provisions and as many goods as they could carry and found that prices were rising. Local provision shops opened far beyond their usual closing times. Although the Government maximum-price scheme quickly put a stop to it, the price of sugar immediately went up and the Government had to issue suggested prices for it and hoarding was made a criminal offence.

Within hours, the suffragettes put their aims on hold. Leaders of the women's suffrage movement supported the war effort, urging men to enlist and women to work in industry, preferring to put temporarily aside their cause. It also worked to combat the appalling poverty suffered by ordinary people.

Boy scouts, some of whom were in camp, were urgently summoned back. Army units mustered in camps were immediately put on a war footing. Others en route for their annual camp were stopped mid journey, their trains turned round to return to London. Patriotic fever gripped the whole country. The local volunteers of 'E' Company, 8th Middlesex V.B. Regiment returned home on 4th August. Two or three days later the men left for Hounslow, were first stationed at Sittingbourne and subsequently transferred, to their great disappointment, to Gibraltar for 5 months after which they were relieved by their second-line battalions and saw service in France. Men who more often than not had ventured no more than a few miles from their homes were soon to find themselves in France or Flanders – or even further afield. On 7th August 1914, the first details of the British Army – the 'Old Contemptibles' came down the gangway from a troopship at Boulogne – this time not as foes, but as allies.

Every farm had its hayricks commandeered by the War Department, leaving only the bare minimum. Hay was baled by the Pioneer Corps and taken away to Cavalry depots. The authorities had lists of all tradesmen and others who were likely to be able to furnish draught and other horses and the War Office commandeered several horses from local traders. In one instance a pair of horses was commandeered on the Bath Road by the military authorities who immediately took them from the carriage. Local Councils at first found it very difficult to get supplies as local traders had had their horses taken from them for military purposes, but they quickly set up Emergency Committees for arranging relief measures for those on active service and their dependents.

St. Dunstan's Church, Cranford
(Hillingdon Local Studies. Archives and Museum Service)

In Yeading at the outbreak of war almost all the land at Manor Farm was requisitioned by the War Department. It was handed back in 1918 only to be requisitioned again in 1939.

All building work ceased and although the Middlesex County Council took steps to purchase building material, the labour required to construct the Great West Road was not available as men were called up and until 1919 all other operations apart from acquisitions of land were suspended.

Several residents were holidaying or working abroad and arrived home with fascinating stories to tell. Two former residents of Hayes, the sister and niece of the late Dr. Hunter had been holidaying in Copenhagen, which they left on September 10th 1914 at 8.30am. They arrived in Newcastle after a stirring journey from Norway, during which time they had been twice stopped by British war ships and boarded by officers and men who searched the ship, while the ladies from the port-holes admired the battleships and destroyers, looking like 'faithful watch dogs of the deep'.

A policy adopted by the railway companies was that, on the advent of war, platelayers and others of their employees would watch and patrol, both by day and by night, the lines over which troop trains might be expected to pass.

Local Councils, along with other employers, found business difficult with prices rising, supplies drying up, men joining up and transport being requisitioned by the Government, but quickly set up Emergency Committees for arranging relief measures for those on active service. Several traders cancelled their contracts with the Council as they had great difficulty in getting their supplies. Council employees were guaranteed their jobs if and when they returned from the war. They also were to receive the wages they earned when they left the Council to join up, minus their Army, Navy or Air Force pay.

The conflict, which was to be one of the greatest in the history of the world, was to grow to involve the whole population.

RECRUITMENT
In the beginning, Britain's forces were composed of regular soldiers, Territorials and Volunteers. In August 1914, Britain had only a small professional army of about 150,000 men. Britain alone relied entirely on volunteers. Lord Kitchener, Secretary of War, thrice appealed for 100,000 volunteers in August and September 1914 and floods of volunteers came forward. Fathers, sons and

husbands went off the war, in many cases driven by unemployment. Before the war was six months old, more men from Britain and the British Empire were under arms than any time in history.

The Parliamentary Recruiting Committee for the Uxbridge Division was arranged in District Advisory Sub-Committees. The Uxbridge recruiting area covered Uxbridge Urban, Hillingdon, Hayes, Northolt, Ickenham, Cowley and Yiewsley and there were also Canvassing Sub-Committees. In early 1915, Colonel Carr-Calthrop, honorary recruiting officer, was brought on the recruiting staff of No. 10 military district. His sub-areas included Ealing, Hanwell, Greenford, Perivale, Southall, Hayes and Northolt.

Initial enlistments were carried out by the Army's own Recruiting Service, at the depots and the regular recruiting offices, council offices, or at a hastily opened temporary office, such as schools and business premises. Staines RDC covered Harlington, Harmondsworth, Cranford, Ashford, Bedfont, Stanwell and Shepperton. Recruiting for the Harmondsworth, Cranford and Harlington areas was mostly at Hounslow Barracks and most men who enlisted there served in the Royal Fusiliers. On 1st December 1915 a 'special day' was provided by Major Davies of Staines for Harlington men to become attested

In mid August 1914 the Uxbridge and District Emergency Committee issued an appeal in support of Lord Kitchener's second army of 100,00 men. A few days after war was declared the first recruiting appeal posters appeared in the district. Recruiting Smoking Concerts began to be held and went on throughout hostilities. Other forms of recruitment also took place

The Territorials came into being in 1908 formed from existing volunteer units- "weekend" soldiers so vitally important at a time when the regular army had undergone such huge reductions. Territorials were only intended for home defence unless they personally volunteered to do otherwise, although by 1915 many Territorial battalions were at the Front. There had been a surplus of volunteers who had sought to enlist, but the 8th Middlesex Regiment with its full complement of men along with other regiments from the regular and Territorial Army had departed for war in early September 1914. In their place one thousand West Middlesex men eagerly joined the new Territorial force, the 8th (Reserve) Battalion Middlesex Regiment. The Company left in September 1914 for their training quarters at Hampton Court. A huge crowd gathered at Uxbridge station to bid them farewell. Shortly afterwards a 2nd Reserve Battalion, the 2/8th Middlesex was called for. Young Captain (later Major) John Aubrey Down of the 'E' Company of the Uxbridge Territorials, was selected to form the new battalion. He all but commandeered the Gazette's Uxbridge, Southall, Ealing, Hanwell and Acton offices as well as a handful of local shops as recruitment centres and within four days a battalion was raised. Recruiting for the Middlesex Territorial force took a very large number of men from the district as did the Royal Fusiliers. Between August 12th 1914 and October 11th 1915, a total of 855 recruits had enlisted at Uxbridge and in March 1915 it was reported in the local paper that recruitment in the Uxbridge district was going smoothly and young men were still coming forward to enlist in both Kitchener's Army and the new Territorial Battalion, the 3/8th

Middlesex. On one Sunday in mid March 1915 a vigorous campaign had been conducted for recruitment to this new Territorial Battalion. A fleet of cars with speakers, recruiters and the Southall Town Band set off from Southall scouring the district, visiting Hayes, Harlington and Hillingdon. Doctors Davidson, Francis, Lock and Walker medically examined the men. The 4/8th Middlesex (Territorial) Regiment was raised in July 1915. Many Cadet Corps were formed.

There were numerous local men who were Reservists, former soldiers and sailors serving their 7 years' reserve commitment. In the first week of war nineteen army Reservists from the Great Western railway sleeper pickling yard at Botwell answered the call of duty. Notices placed in local Post Offices by the police were the usual way Reserves were recalled. In the first week of war nineteen army Reservists from the Great Western railway sleeper pickling yard at Botwell answered the call of duty. Notices placed in local Post Offices by the police were the usual way Reserves were recalled. P.C.Ogden of Hayes, who at the outbreak of war rejoined the Navy and was one who took part in the Jutland Naval Battle on HMS '*Falmouth*'. George Dowman, son of Mr. and Mrs Dowman of Wood End Green, was another reservist, joining when war began in the 2nd Highland Light Infantry.

By late 1914, recruitment numbers had fallen everywhere and continuing efforts were made to recruit more men, but as the lists of those killed in action or wounded grew ever-longer, understandably there was a lot of antipathy. By November 1915, already 13 residents of Hayes had been killed in action. The National Register had started in about August 1915 and completed with certificates of registration issued by the end of the month. Every citizen aged between 16 and 65 had to supply details of age, sex and occupation and whether or not they would perform work of national importance. It was not meant as an aid to recruitment but was ultimately used as such.

In a final effort to save voluntary conscription, the Government introduced the 'Derby Scheme'. Lord Derby was appointed National Director-General of Recruiting in October 1915 resulting in more systematic recruitment. On the basis of a National Register, every man between 18 and 41 was called up in groups as they were wanted, taking the younger single man first. However, although there had been a huge number of volunteers, this scheme was not successful and by May 1916 conscription was brought in, although men could still enlist voluntarily. Britain was by now fighting in western Europe, Turkey, the Middle East and Italy and the losses on the Somme, the bloodiest day in the history of British warfare, put the pressure on for more recruits.

Also under Lord Derby's scheme of 1915 the basic principle for non-enlistment was that it was the State to say whether or not a man was indispensable. The various authorities interested, always with a military representative, were empowered to decide. In late October 1916, the Urban District of Hayes received a letter from the Local Government Board requesting the Council to appoint, without delay, a Local Tribunal of 5 members who would have the power to adjudicate on cases arising out of the Recruiting Scheme under the control of Lord Derby. A local Tribunal was duly appointed, which met under the chairman, Mr. J. Ellis, at the

Council Offices at 6.30 in the evening as and when. Mr. R.W. Gunton was also a member of the Hayes Local Tribunal which had its inaugural meeting on 23rd December 1915. The Military Representative objected to his presence because he was of Military age and may be biased towards men of his own age. The Tribunal decided that he could remain in office until he resigned voluntarily, but although Mr. Gunton expressed his intention of remaining on the Tribunal, the M.R. notified the Tribunal of his intention to proceed with his objection further. There is no further reference to him after the meeting of 26th January 1916.

Military Tribunals were set up in every Borough under the Military Service Act 1916, which were aimed at forcing unmarried men to do what they had hitherto failed to do at Lord Derby's invitation, to hear the appeals of men or local employers who could not or would not join up for reasons of occupation, religious belief, hardship or conscience. The Military Tribunals could grant temporary exemptions on condition that the applicant joined the Special Constables, VTC where they were to undertake a specified number of drills, the Motor Volunteer Corps or went to work in munitions. Most exemption claims came from employers seeking immunity for their employees on the grounds of indispensability. A large number came from men engaged as market gardeners or in other forms of agriculture or those already working in munitions. It was not uncommon to find that at some of these appeals young to youngish local farmers were told to go to the Military Barracks at Hounslow to look for replacements.

Conscientious Objectors groups sprang up all over the country. Messrs. Harrison and Sons put in a claim for Percy James at the Military Tribunal at Hayes on 17th January 1916, which was postponed until 8th March 1916. When he reappeared he claimed he was a conscientious objector. His claim was dismissed. In the spring of 1916, the Committee on Work of National Importance which was responsible for finding suitable work for conscientious objectors to military service wrote to the Middlesex County Council inviting them to fill vacancies on its staff with such men. The MCC with indignance and without much discussion agreed that conscientious objectors should not be employed in any capacity by the County Council.

The Hayes Urban Military Tribunal convened at the Council offices. Harlington, Dawley and Cranford came under the Staines Rural and were held at Stanwell. As its name suggests, the Middlesex County Appeals Tribunal heard appeals. They were harsh. In one instance a forty year old widower with one child who lived with his mother, the licensee of a public house in Hayes, appealed for an exemption on the grounds of his business of carter and contractor with market gardening. He employed two men to take the produce to Brentford market in his own horse and cart. He was given two weeks to dispose of his business.

About 400 individual cases were heard at Uxbridge and altogether 463 were heard at Hayes. These Tribunals, most of which were unsuccessful, were abolished in October 1918.

In a desperate attempt to recruit more soldiers a Military Service Act was passed in mid-April 1918 – hurriedly allowing the conscription of men up to the age of 51, regardless of the effect on industrial output.

Thousands of expatriates rushed to their mother countries to join the crusade. Twelve other Frenchmen in the Botwell area left immediately war was declared to join the French Army. Frank Shackle, the only son of Frank Shackle of Hayes had gone to Canada after leaving Haileybury School. He returned to England on the outbreak of war and entered Sandhurst. He was commissioned in the Middlesex Regiment as Captain and Adjutant, and was killed by a shell on 21st November 1917, aged 27. Many others who had emigrated also answered the call in their adopted country.

In mid August 1914, 100 Army and Navy Reservists left Harlington for the war in one week. By the first week of September 1914, 9 men from Hayes and Harlington had joined the Navy and over 50 had joined the Army and by April 1915, about 200 men from the parish had enlisted. Up to late 1915, 85 men from Cranford had joined one or other of the forces. Forty 'old boys' from Hayes Jewish School had enlisted by February 1915. By the end of 1916, almost 250 men from Hayes had joined up. In the spring of 1917 the Council erected a board outside the Council offices showing the names of all the residents of Hayes who were serving with HM Forces.

EMPLOYMENT

By the second week of war, the future for the industries based at Hayes looked bleak and many unfounded rumours circulated. It was feared that some Hayes factories would have to close because of the effect the war was having on them. In some cases men were turned away because of the lack of work, others were working three-quarter time, while others were working three days a week and some half days only. Belgian and other refugees were gradually arriving and by September 1914 those able to work had signed on at the Labour Exchanges. Admiralty and War Office contractors were given instructions that any Belgian labour should be engaged through the Labour Exchanges.

The Army Motor Lorries and Waggon Co. Limited in 1915 (Hillingdon Local Studies, Archives and Museum Service)

The British Electric Transformer Co. Ltd., workforce was working a short week. Both Goss and Orchestrelle were working short weeks, but by the early weeks of the war practically the whole Orchestrelle works was closed with only a few departments working. Harrison's printers found that they could not obtain certain dyestuffs for some of their stamps which they had hitherto obtained from Germany. The declaration of war coincided with the Gramophone Company's long-planned commencement of gramophone manufacture, but these plans were put on hold and rather than the anticipated boom in sales in the 1914-15 season, the Gramophone Company almost foundered. The throbbing engines were silent and the place almost deserted. A rumour spread that the whole works had closed down. It was estimated that 3,000 people failed to find work at Hayes. Several of them undertook sewage work at Yeading.

However, the initial rise in unemployment and poverty was brief and as the war continued the demand for war material increased. Gradually many existing factories converted all or part of their production lines to the making of war materials, under the Defence of the Realm Act. This Act enabled the Government to take over and use any factory or workshop anywhere, control its processes and output, to remove its plant elsewhere if necessary, to commandeer empty property for housing workmen engaged on war work, and to annul any contracts which stood in the way of firms carrying out the production of war material. In 1915, the Metropolitan Munitions Committee was set up in Kingsway to further the output of war material in the Metropolitan area, which itself was divided into areas. Its brief was to determine what in each district was capable of production, obtaining help from suitable traders and others, as well as determining which new works or shops should be rented or bought. They also had full powers to rent lathes, machine tools, presses etc of those at that time who were engaged on civil work in the Metropolitan area, but any purchase had to be agreed with the Ministry of Munitions.

Many factories made very extensive additions, the like of which would not have been seen but for the urgent requirements of the war departments. Local saddlers made harnesses and motor car shops and the engineers obtained contracts suitable to their line of work. Every available lathe was put to turning shells - if an employer was willing to use his lathe for that purpose he was allowed to keep it in his own workshop and employ his own workers, if not his lathe was commandeered and taken off for use in some other workshop. There was evidence that some firms who had been doing commercial work and who wanted their men to stay with them took up munitions in order to retain their men. It could be said that Great Britain was for the first time under the thumb of Government Departments. At the end of 1914, the percentage of unemployed was the lowest on record and the unemployment parades had ceased – at last there was work for everybody but everywhere there was a feeling of urgency.

At the British Electric Transformer Co. Ltd., the workforce was back working full-time employed with plenty of supplies including some important Government wireless work in early September 1914. It was still employed in important Government work in 1918. In August of that year, Ealing Local Tribunal had given Mr. J. Nye exemption on condition that he undertook work of national importance. It seems that Mr. Nye was working for the British Electric Transformer Co., but was sent to work at the Gramophone Company. The British Transformer Company sent Ealing Tribunal a strongly worded protest as they were still engaged on important Government work. In July 1915 an Act of Parliament had laid down that a munitions worker could not be taken on by another firm within six weeks of leaving his last job, unless he had a leaving certificate from them. This was to try and stop 'poaching'. This approach was abandoned in July 1917. By late August 1914, the X-Chair Company had received a very large

Army contract, but were worried how to transport the goods to their destination, and by 1916 was engaged on work of direct use to the troops and to the nurses of the various hospital units. Sometime later Orchestrelle's piano and music roll factories were engaged for making aeroplane parts, detonator cases for the Navy, hand grenades, munitions boxes and metal tobacco boxes for the forces. In late 1916 a shed was constructed for munition transit boxes. By 1917, the Orchestrelle Company had changed its name to the Aeolian Company and had been extended. A temporary shed was erected for war purposes in early 1918 and further extensions were made to an existing building in mid 1918 for aeroplane work on the premises. Amongst other things, it also made fuses.

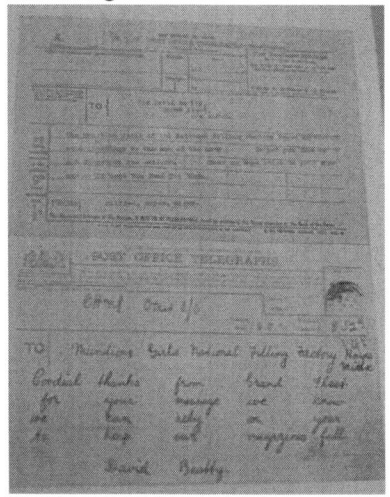

Facsimile of a telegram sent to Sir David Beatty from the Factory at Easter 1918 and his reply. (Hillingdon Local Studies, Archives and Museum Service)

The production of aeroplane engines was limited due to the supply of skilled labour. As a result of the reorganisation of existing facilities to increase production, which was urgently required, in early 1917 the Goss Printing Press factory and land in Blyth Road was purchased and in the following October became the National Aero-engine Factory, a controlled establishment under the Air Board. It manufactured aeroplane engines and spares of numerous types and also carried out experimental work for the Ministry of Munitions of War from January 1917 to the end of the War. In the beginning, there was a dispute as to who actually owned the property, which ended in October 1917 when the management, Messrs. Mitchell, Shaw and Co. were either dismissed by the Ministry for misconduct or resigned for sloppy workmanship and the factory declared the absolute property of the Government and the rates of pay established Although negotiations were suspended at this time, work carried on and after the change in management, the production improved. The property was extended in late 1917 but was not carried out in accordance with the Byelaws, however it appears to have remained. Although labour disputes were a constant source of worry in National Aircraft Factories, they were a rare occurrence at Hayes, thought to be put down to the fact that it was Government controlled and their wages in excess of the London district rates, which had been set in October 1917, much to the annoyance of neighbouring factories. In June 1918 the factory was organised specially to deal with urgent requirements and skilled labour was essential. 761 employees, 213 of whom where women, were working there by October 1918. The factory was sold in September 1919. By mid August 1915 Sandow's Cocoa and Chocolate Ltd. was working full-time on a Government contract, but in the autumn of 1916 it had gone into compulsory liquidation and taken over by the Hayes Cocoa Co., which by late 1917 was on a limited arms contract.

Harrison's Printing Works continued to have difficulty in producing stamps of certain values and colours and as time went on, this shortage became more acute and by 1916 it was so bad that the production of some stamps was almost discontinued. In order to partially overcome this problem, in 1915 the Government had set up British Dyes Ltd., with a factory in Huddersfield to produce various pigments, although its main purpose was to make TNT. Harrisons had also managed to obtain suitable colours from seized materials and by mid 1917 were again producing all stamps for the Government.

Three Belgians with a small nominal capital (£1,600) formed the Army Motor Lorries and Waggon Co. Limited in London in 1914. The company was contracted to the Belgian War Office to provide munitions and also received orders from the British Government. In October 1914 the new company moved into premises on about four acres that had formerly belonged to Arthur Lee and Brothers Limited, a marble-making firm, in Clayton Road, Hayes. Minimal alterations had to be made and new buildings (sited near Bourne Bridge in Harlington Parish), some of which were portable, had to be erected quickly to cope with the demand. Machinery was installed for the special purpose of manufacturing armoured cars. Huge sheds were also erected for the storage of wood, which mainly came from Russia. The Company also acquired a large wooden shed in North Hyde Road. 350 workers, as many as half of whom were Belgian refugees, came from the surrounding areas and further afield aggravating the shortage of housing in the district. Two brothers, Lucien and Leon Bonte had both been partners in a pottery factory at Bruges. They both lodged at Sipson and had attended Uxbridge County School for only a short period, Lucien from 3rd March 1915 until 31st March 1915 and Leon from 3rd March 1915 until 19th March 1915, after which they came to work at the factory. Five male 'guests' at the St. Andrew's hostel at Ealing found work at the factory and were managed to find accommodation after an arduous look. By May 1915 there were over 700 men employed there and much extra land had been acquired. The work there covered a wide field and included the making of cartridge cases and pontoons, in hiring, repairing, cleaning and storing motor lorries, motor cars, motor waggons, carts, trucks, aeroplanes, cycles etc., and vehicles of all kinds. By February 1915 the company was turning out a large number of French artillery limbered waggons (Caisson), armoured cars (Mitralleuse), workshop waggons (Atilier), pontoons and transport. Special bodies supplied by regular motor manufacturers were built onto chassis at Clayton Road, as were units of an automobile field hospital for the Belgian Army. It may also have made artillery carriages. In May 1915 the works presented the Queen of Belgian with a complete field hospital which had been fitted with the most up-to-date equipment. The equipment for this field hospital, which had been subscribed to by Belgian workers in England, included X-Ray units, a kitchen and generators. The labour force eventually reached 5,000-6,000 men. Children from Clayton Road School were asked to help find lodgings for the workers.

The Beck Engineering Company at Hayes End obtained an order from the Government in September 1915 for the supply of one million friction tubes, but was unable to provide the necessary funds to undertake the work. The AMB Syndicate Ltd. agreed to provide a loan. The Company agreed to provide the necessary labour and materials at cost price and the Syndicate was to pay the company 1½d. per friction tube accepted by the Government. In November 1915 the Company obtained a munitions contract to supply a large number of primers for cartridge cases. In order to manufacture the primers, the company needed certain machinery and plant and also an extension to the building. They obtained a loan of £10,000, which was to be repaid by July 1916, with 25 per cent of the total net profits arising from the contracts. Between April 1915 and August 1916 the Company made a loss on trading whereupon a receiver was appointed by the debenture holders. It was liquidated in 1920.

The Army Motor Lorries Company had use for only half the factory and in mid 1915 the wartime Government found Richard Fairey his own factory in the Clayton Road site. Fairey Aviation Company took a lease on the premises and the large wooden shed, and produced aircraft for the Government. They also repaired and modified aeroplanes here, e.g. a Curtis Biplane was repaired at Fairey's in early September 1915 and a Sopwith Strutter damaged at Manston in June 1916 was also repaired here. Deliveries to and from the factory were by road. Some of the AMLC's skilled workers were also available to Fairey who were contracted to build twelve Short 827 seaplanes. A field at Harlington near to the Great Western Railway main line to Reading and Oxford was purchased and a hangar built or converted for the assembly of the seaplanes. A two-storey building adjoined the experimental and assembly sheds included a drawing office, main building and a fabric/dope shop. Female staff were also employed here. Northolt Aerodrome was used as a testing ground for the engines and planes. Land at West Drayton, which bordered on the edge of the Grand Junction Canal and the GWR railway, was taken under the Defence of the Realm Act, for war purposes by the Air Ministry in late November 1917. Here buildings were constructed for a Stores Depot attached to the Armament and Gunnery School at Uxbridge. It was also used to store and service aircraft engines manufactured by Fairey at Hayes.

Fairey himself had been seconded to EMI for a short time until setting up his own company. The success of Fairey's Short seaplanes gave the new company recognition, which was realised by mid 1916 when Fairey obtained a contract for 100 Sopwith 1½ Strutters for the RNAS. Work on these started in October 1916 at Clayton Road and all were produced in less than a year, 26 in 1916 and the remainder by September 1917. Initial test flying was carried out from a field adjacent to the factory and later they were flown from Kingsbury airfield, which no longer exists, as well as from Northolt. Financial irregularities led to the Army Motor Lorries and Waggon Company winding up (voluntary liquidation) in January 1916, whereupon Fairey Aviation acquired the Clayton Road factory. Also in 1916, Fairey's first seaplane, the Hamble Baby, which was based on the Sopwith Baby but with floats, was constructed followed by the Campania, a two-seat patrol seaplane designed in 1916 for reconnaissance purposes with the Fleet and to meet an Admiralty specification for operations from carrier vessels, in particular a converted passenger liner, the HMS *'Campania'*. However, it was found that seaplanes were not well adapted for use with the Fleet. One of Fairey's Campania seaplanes, which had been built at Hayes but erected and tested at Hamble, near Southampton, dropped 2 x 230lb bombs on a suspected U-Boat in mid May 1918. The Fairey F.2 was a biplane, built at Hayes, with 2 Rolls Royce engines, one Lewis gun and collapsible wings. The prototype's first flight was at Northolt on 17th May 1917 after which the Admiralty became disinterested in the project. It would have been capable of intercepting alien aeroplanes and Zeppelins.

  Although the assembly building at Harlington had been extended, by 1917 there was an urgent need for additional factory area and larger assembly shops. A Government loan of £20,000 was made available and a plant was built on the Harlington site to the south of the Great Western Railway near Hayes. Work started in autumn 1917 and it was ready by the spring of 1918 and continued to be the site of Fairey's headquarters during the life of the company. The buildings included an erecting shop with a 90ft. span and a height of 24ft., together with assembly bays and fitting and machine shops. In August 1917 Hayes UDC corresponded with the Munitions Work Board with regard to the connection of the Harlington premises to the Hayes sewerage scheme. The Board was prepared to recommend a loan for the extension of the Disposal Works and 5%, if the Council would accept the sewage from the factory. At first the Council drew to the Board's attention that there was an outstanding grant in aid of rates in connection with the Filling Factory No. 7. Once that was dealt with, the Council would then be prepared to enter into negotiations for the reception of waste water from Fairey's, on the basis that the Ministry of Munitions made good a grant of two-thirds of the total cost of the extensions to the Sewage Disposal Works and the whole cost of the additional pumping plant which was required. The Munitions Work Board agreed to the Council's request for the pumping plant.

Fifty Fairey IIIAs were built at Hayes in 1918 for the RNAS which was then about to be merged with the RFC to form the RAF. They were intended as replacements for the obsolete Sopwith 1½ Strutters. 100 Sopwith 2F.1 Ship's Camel Tractor Biplane Scouts, numbered N7200-N7299 were ordered from Faireys, to be built at Hayes in late 1918, but these were cancelled in November 1918. At about the same time, thirty Fairey IIIB Tractor Biplane Seaplanes were ordered under the numbers N9230 to N9259 to be built at Hayes but these were all delivered after the end of hostilities. It is amazing to think that 24 years later a variation of the IIIB, the Fairey IIIF biplanes, were still on active service.

Smaller firms in the area were also engaged in Government contract work. An English timber merchant of Hayes employed 14 men and 2 boys for the work. At Harlington the proprietor of an ironworks described himself as an inventor and sole proprietor of a secret process for recovering from waste high-grade steel used in munition work. In the autumn of 1916 he convinced the local Military Tribunal to give him a conditional exemption.

The inadequate supply of munitions caused by the shortage of cordite, which was used for firing artillery shells, had by 1915 become a most pressing question and contractors on War Office work had failed to deliver only a third of the number of shells required. At the end of May 1915 a raw materials branch set up by the Admiralty and the War Office dealt with the supply of raw and semi-manufactures materials for shell-making. In truth, the Government were well aware of the situation after the Battle of the Aisne in September 1914 –there was a serious shortage of shells on both the Western and Eastern fronts. During the whole of the 2¾ years of the Boer War, the amount of ammunition expended was not much more than was spent by our artillery alone in a fortnight in and around Neuve Chapelle in March 1915. At Ypres in the April of 1915, the heavy losses and expenditure of an already none too plentiful amount of ammunition was jeopardising future engagements. Our guns were only able to fire 12 shells a day to the German 100. In March of that year Lloyd George had been bombarded by the House about the drastic provision in his Bill for the taking over of factories to make war material. By May 1915, the Government was still debating the situation. This procrastination ended when the Ministry of Munitions Act was laid before Parliament at the beginning of June 1915. Christopher Addison of Northwood was appointed parliamentary secretary, chiefly in charge of supply. Munition production increased and private enterprise was brought under Government control. By 1915 night shifts at factories, which were working at very high pressure, were commonplace.

Between 1915 and 1917 several large munitions factories and depots were constructed. Some new buildings sprang up whilst other existing factories made very extensive additions to fulfil the urgent requirements of the War Department. By the end of the war there were 15 National Projectile Factories for the production of heavy shells, 15 National Filling Factories where empty shell cases were filled with explosive and 4 National Cartridge Factories to supply rifle ammunition.

The Universal Music Company in Silverdale Road began munition work and in the spring of 1916 erected a temporary building particularly for war munitions purposes.

To ensure the Company's survival, the Gramophone Company had made drastic economies and dismissed a large number of staff. The staff left took a 25% reduction in their wages and war-related munitions contracts were obtained under Government control. Plans were approved for a temporary extension in mid-November 1914 so that part of the works could be converted to produce munitions. By early 1915 extensions were being carried out at night by means of an electric light. Acres of land were covered with buildings making munitions and aeroplane parts. The Works were by now huge. Since the beginning of the war, the Company had imported 15,000 tons of metal and by June 1915, the Gramophone factory, which became a 'controlled company' on 6th September 1915 (No. 8 Filling Factory) employed around 4,000 workers on making munitions, from chargers, primers, pull-through weights, ammunition boxes, shell cases, cartridge cases, time-fuses to aeroplane parts. In 1915, the Company became suppliers of material to the Metropolitan Munitions Committee and in November 1915 the Company was reported to have made large profits. By late 1916 the Church Army was running a large canteen for munition workers at the works which could hold between 600 and 700 men. Harry Lauder, who was famous all the world over for his Scottish songs visited the Company on at least two occasions, the second in the spring of 1915. In the spring of 1917 the King and Queen paid an informal visit to the Gramophone Company premises and other Hayes and Botwell factories. The wartime output for the Government was 7,100,000 brass shell cases (mostly of the 18-pounder type), 5,500,000 cartridge cases, 4,000,000 time fuses (each having some 30 different parts to be assembled), 19,200,000 primers, 127,000,000 cartridge charger clips, 1,500,000 pull-through weights for rifles and a great number of aeroplane parts and tools and equipment for other factories. The cabinet factory made over 4,500 complete aeroplanes and a number of parts as well as 500,000 ammunition boxes, which utilized 7,000 tons of timber. The production of gramophone records continued, albeit somewhat curtailed, despite the fact that the enemy tried to pass information from one country to another by means of records and in total 17,000,000 records were produced. Recordings were largely devoted to morale-boosting songs recorded for the troops by the famous music-hall stars of the time. Throughout the war, the British record industry as a whole saw a significant growth. In part, this growth was caused by the unavailability of German manufactured records which before the outbreak of hostilities had captured half the British market. The biggest boost, however, came from the trenches as well as from the home front. By the end of the war, the Gramophone Company's sales for October 1918 had exceeded any month hitherto but had lost its German business and was never able to regain control of it.

  In mid 1915 Lloyd George, as Minister of Munitions, decided that large factories for filling munitions were to be built within 20 miles of London. Hayes was decided upon as it satisfied a number of requirements. The site was chosen by Mr. A.C. Blyth, at the request of the Ministry of Munitions, who had investigated many of the London sites, as it was large enough, close to a water supply and transport and near to residential areas. This latter requisite was considered a necessity as it was thought that most of the workers would be women and the Ministry wanted to avoid at all costs taking them away from their homes and having to control them after working hours.

Hayes Filling Factory Ambulance (Hillingdon Local Studies, Archives and Museum Service)

The work was also of a less dangerous nature than other filling operations and could be carried out in more closely populated areas. Mr. Blyth later became the factory manager of both the Hayes and the Sumner Street (Southwark) factories, and remained as such throughout the war until the Armistice. The Sumner Street factory, built on unoccupied land of which the title was in dispute, was a subsidiary of the Hayes factory for a time. The factory at Sumner Street filled shell components and from 1918 also inspected protective clothing. The north side of the Hayes factory adjoined the Slough line of the Great Western Railway and to its north-eastern boundary was the Grand Junction Canal. Just over a mile away was the main Uxbridge to London road and two miles away was the Bath Road.

Female munitions workers at Hayes (Hillingdon Local Studies, Archives and Museum Service)

Construction started on 'The Factory in the Fields' or 'Tin Town' as the National Filling Factory No. 7 was known, on this site on 18th September 1915. It was administered directly under the Ministry of Munitions and was intended to be one of the six factories assembling and filling various classes of gun ammunition components. It was erected by the London firm of Messrs. Higgs and Hill and was a temporary factory with 397 buildings, divided into 5 sections, with a total floor area of 14 acres. The Ministry of Munitions' Machine Tool Department had set up a small tools section in September 1915 which provided the small tools to the National Shell, Projectile, Fuse and Filling Factories. The factory was on a large site adjoining Sandow's factory and comprised almost 200 acres south of the railway, part of which had previously been a market garden and fields. Timber for the factory was purchased by the shipload. Unfortunately two cargoes were sunk by U-boats. Shell filling (block-filling of 18 pounder shells) commenced on 30th October 1915. It was the first Filling Factory to begin production, apart from the emergency unit at Southwark.

The Factory in the Fields.

'The Factory in the Fields' Hillingdon Local Studies, Archives and Museum Service)

The factory was situated in the south-east corner of Hayes and extended south from Nestle's Avenue, across North Hyde Road to Cranford Park. The main entrance was only 200 yards from Hayes and Harlington station. Other entrances included one half-way down the station bridge and another the far end of North Hyde Road, near the Watersplash on the eastern boundary, where a ford crossed the River Crane on the road to Southall. Each entrance was guarded by a sentry in a sentry box. A 10-foot high corrugated iron fence surrounded it. The factory's military guard consisted of a colonel, a captain, three subalterns and 190 NCOs and men. There were also 40 watchmen who patrolled the factory by night. No unrecognised person was allowed to enter the factory.

The buildings were raised above the ground by concrete pillars and connecting each building was a small railway laid on a raised platform to the same height of the workshops. The total length of these platforms was over 15 miles. Rules were laid down which had to be strictly observed. Boxes to be sent direct to the front were packed in smaller shops.

The Great Western Railway Company scheduled a strip of land about 100 feet wide alongside their line at Hayes for compulsory purchase for the purpose of widening their line and the vacant portion of the site was commandeered by the Government for military purposes for the period of hostilities. To this end a railway siding was put in which enabled trains to run straight into the factory, with the possible idea that it would be available for ordinary goods traffic when the Government relinquished the property.

The red-bricked chimney of the Hayes Cocoa Company stood right in the midst of the filling sheds. The sheds, which were heated with steam and the temperature carefully regulated, were widely separated and connected with wooden walkways to diminish the risk of a major explosion. Only a limited amount of explosive was allowed in one shop at a time.

The Inland Waterways and Docks Directorate, although not manned by its personnel, conveyed ammunition between Dagenham Docks, where there was a National Cartridge and Box Repair Factory, and Hayes. Barges were unloaded on the site. Special Great Western Railway trains conveying shells ran daily from Hayes to Southampton and Richborough, a new port constructed during the war, which dispatched 10,000 barges carrying 650,000 tons of ammunition and 11,000 guns. The average number of wagons dealt with per month was about 3,800. In 1916 shells were also dispatched to Liverpool, although this may also have been the case previously. Motorized lorries and steam wagons also brought material from local depots and motor cars were also used to dispatch shells to various stations.

In November 1915, the managing director was given instructions to plan an extension to the factory to include a shell-filling unit, which took over a proportion of what would have been produced at a filling factory at Watford which was not built. The new unit was capable of manufacturing and filling into shell 200 tons of amatol per week and 100 tons of lyddite.

During 1915 and 1916, a very considerable capacity for the manufacture of amatol was established by installing drying and mixing plant in the new National Filling Factories as the transportation of amatol from factory to filling stations would have been very difficult. The factory was for component and shell filling, compressing the explosives, filling gaines (tubes filled with explosives attached under the nose-cap of a high-explosive shell and sticking down into the TNT filling) and such other work as may be determined from time to time. In late November 1915 Hayes Council applied to the Ministry of Munitions for a grant towards the damage done to Coldharbour Lane during construction of the factory, which, with another munitions factory at Park Royal (The 'Perivale' Filling Factory), was at that time the largest in the country.

Apart from shell filling, other duties were carried out including making cartridges and assembling 18-pounders. This took place for a time in the West Section until the production of 18-pounder light shells was curtailed in the spring of 1916, in order to release steel for larger shells, although later on in the war these 18 pounders were made again.

. By the end of 1915 Hayes and the factory at Devonport together had assembled 73,600 rounds of 18- pounder ammunition. Shell filling took place in the larger shops, which were further apart. Here gloves were worn to protect hands from rough metal and gauze respirators were provided against the chemical-laden dust.

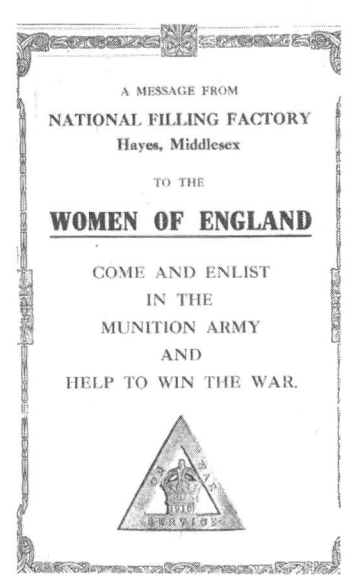

A MESSAGE FROM
NATIONAL FILLING FACTORY
Hayes, Middlesex

TO THE
WOMEN OF ENGLAND

COME AND ENLIST
IN THE
MUNITION ARMY
AND
HELP TO WIN THE WAR.

(Gazette newspapers)

When Southwark ceased to fill gaines towards the end of 1915, the work was undertaken at Hayes. In late September 1915, the filling of gaines, primers, T. tubes and detonators began and in October that same year fuse-filling commenced. In mid January 1916 time fuses ceased to be made at Hayes and in April 1916 they started making anti-aircraft ammunition. The factory was given specific Allocations to meet. For example the Allocation on the last day of January 1916 was for 1,000 high explosive shells (60 pounder HE shell Amatol 40/60) and 2,000 x 60 pounder cordite (known in common parlance as devil's porridge) cartridges.

A week later instructions followed to make the same number of HE shells but to raise the number of other shells (QF 4.7 MK VIII shells) from 1,050 to

2,000 per week. Throughout the country, between 1st March 1918 and 1st August 1918, the production of all munitions was drastically improved. The strength of the Tank Corps increased by 27% and that of the Machine Gun Corps by 41%, while the number of aeroplanes in France rose by 40%.

During the first month on the battle of the Somme in July 1916, the expenditure in shells was almost 50% greater than the quantity landed in France during the same period and as the demand for shells continued unabated, more and more tin huts sprang up.

By January 1918 there was an urgent need for more chemical projectiles, the use of which had been approved in the spring of 1916. Because of the lack of railway sidings at the Greenford chemical shell-filling factory, it was impossible to extend the factory further. In July of 1918, the filling station at Banbury forwarded over 200,000 x 18-pounder shells to Hayes and the factory at Hereford forwarded about 1,000 x 18-pounder shells to Hayes. All were mustard gas shells. This work at Hayes commenced on 19th August 1918 and the total number assembled was just over 200,000 x 18-pounders.

At first the explosives were stored on the site in 5 magazines, but as the factory increased in size and output, it was decided to store the explosives en bloc, some way away from the site. A large storage depot in South Ruislip, but named after the nearby Northolt Junction station, although actually outside that parish, was constructed by Higgs and Hill in late 1916 on the east side of West End Road, opposite Northolt Aerodrome, and stretched almost as far as Ruislip Manor and Eastcote, covering Bessingby Park. It consisted of 20 huts spaced far apart.

Explosives for the factory were stored here and each magazine could hold 100 tons of explosives. Communications links were also made between the two sites by the nearby road and by rail – the Great Western and the Great Central Railways. There were also smaller storage depots for fuses, cases of primer etc., at Hayes (No. 84), at Rubastic Road in Southall (No, 3) and at No. 74 Store at Norwood Mills. Daily deliveries were made to the Hayes factory.

Just before the War women had already begun to take up commercial occupations, for instance over 1,000 women already worked in small arms factories and by 1915 women had begun to take on many civilian jobs hitherto thought that only men could do. Munition workers were at first but little affected by conscription as the continual increase in the output of munitions was held to make their retention in the workshops indispensable. Under the voluntary system, it had been necessary to prevent the enlistment of men engaged on vital industrial work.

Gradually, the demands of the army for men made it impossible to keep those less skilled workers who were eligible for military service and could be replaced by women or by men, who for reasons of health or age, were ineligible. Men too old or unfit for service in the army volunteered for work in munitions factories, some even put in long spells of work after working hours. In March 1915, the Board of Trade issued an appeal to all women willing take on any paid employment in any kind of trade, commerce or agriculture to enter their names on a Register of Women for War Service at any employment exchange. After the formation of the Ministry of Munitions in 1915 there was a great extension of the labour of women in the making of war material and munitions factories employed a high percentage of women freeing more men to enlist in the army.

Cartridge Filling at the Hayes Filling Factory. (Hillingdon Local Studies, Archives and Museum Service)

It was estimated that 1,000,000 women worked in these factories and a total of 1,587,300 women had been employed on work directly or indirectly to Government order. In order to work in these factories the applicant had to be in perfect health, supply four references and be of British-born parents. The girls had to be at least 18 years of age. Each was examined prior to being employed and categorized by health conditions and each was then given a unique number.

The flow of women into occupations of an entirely new character and into those, which had formerly been followed by men and boys only, gave rise to difficulties in fixing rates of pay. Orders regulating wages were issued from time to time by the Ministry of Munitions. In 1916 all women's wages in National Factories and controlled establishments were set at 4½d an hour for time workers and 4d an hour for piece workers. At 53 hours this gave women £1.00 weekly whether they were employed in men's work or not. In August 1917 all earnings of women munitions workers were advanced to 2s 6d. Advances on a similar basis were given in December 1917 (3s 6d), in September 1918 (5s), and in January 1919 (5s). Average earnings were considerably higher than these rates and the minimum rate for women on men's work was in January 1919 about three times the general average of women's wages before the War.

10,000 women and more than 2,000 men were employed at the Hayes factory, not including several hundred cleaners etc. At its busiest period, around mid 1916, some 2,500 men were employed at the factory. By now our guns were able to fire 200 to the German 100.

Every worker wore a fireproof overall or tunic suit in khaki, unless working with powders where white trousers and tunics were worn. The clothes were provided in-house. The changing rooms could accommodate up to 7,500 persons at one time. In the Danger Zones, no worker was allowed to step onto the platforms without magazine shoes and no person wearing magazine shoes could step onto the ground. Workshops where the filling took place were 'clean areas'. Stores of empty shell cases as well as the stores of the finished shells were 'dirty areas'.

The working hours were staggered to avoid congestion on the already over-taxed railways. Special trains were arranged for the workers, although many of them cycled in to work. Cycle sheds were provided for them. Working hours were from 6am to 5pm, 7am to 5.30pm or 7.30am to 6pm, with an hours break at midday, although the staff worked in 8-8½ hour shifts day and night. Saturday afternoons were usually a holiday, unless requested to work when extra pay was given, and there was no Sunday working. A fortnight's day work was followed by night work of 10 hours per night for five nights only. Workers had to do their allotted tasks and if they absented themselves without cause, they were brought before Munitions Courts and severely dealt with.

The factory had its own staff of doctors and nurses in attendance. An ambulance was on standby in case of emergencies. The factory also had its own staff of firemen - 60 women! all wearing blue trouser uniforms. Fire-buckets were kept in every shop. Women police were also employed in the factory to control the women workers. There were three large canteens where cheap soup and dinners could be obtained. The cost of building and equipping these canteens was charged against current profits. Princess Marie-Louise of Schleswig-Holstein and Princess Alexandra of Teck had opened a canteen, constructed of corrugated iron, for munitions workers in July 1915 which was run by the Church Army. Mr. A.P. Lethbridge of Redmead Road, Harlington, was a wholesale and retail dairyman who supplied the canteen with milk, butter and eggs – and also with 3,000 gallons of milk per week. There were also rest rooms, one of which was for the women workers. It was built in the grounds of St. Anselm's Church. Some small private temporary shops were opened in the factory grounds. In late 1916 a YWCA hut - a wooden structure- was erected in Keith Road. The main room was the refreshment room which would hold 400 people. There was also a canteen for the men, which was enlarged in 1916 to accommodate 100 customers at a time. In mid 1917 permission was given to the YMCA to make use of a temporary portion of their premises in Keith Road for sleeping accommodation for the duration of the war. By the end of 1916, there was also a canteen at the bottom of Blyth Road. A club for local munitions workers was opened at St. George's parish hall, Southall in late 1916. Opera stars gave lunchtime concerts for the munition workers. Lady Superintendents, who were always on duty in each section, kept lists of local lodgings.

With the numbers of staff rising at a rapid rate, a problem arose with the disposal of waste water. In early 1916 a connection was made in the Council sewers in Cranford Lane for that portion of the factory in the Parish of Harlington. There was a larger ejector in Blyth Road. By mid 1916 the problem had become serious. The Minister of Munitions was contacted and he offered a loan of £300 for the purpose of providing an additional pumping plant driven by electricity for supplementing the efficiency of ejector No 3. The offer was accepted with the proviso that the Minister provided the necessary shed for housing the plant and the facilities for obtaining the necessary land, approximately 20 feet by 20 feet in the neighbourhood of No. 3 ejector.

Filling the shells was very dangerous and risky work and mostly carried out by young women who were mainly from the East End of London, although some local girls were also employed. Training for the work took place in the factory and after two months' experience the workers received a badge inscribed 'On War Service'. The chances of promotion were good. The wages at the Arsenal were good but the work very dangerous and there was an allowance of free milk drunk twice per day to neutralise the effects of the poisonous explosives. They were often called munitionettes, 'canaries' or 'yellow girls' as the TNT powder used to fill the shells, caused fumes which produced symptoms like those of pneumonia and jaundice

The milk allowance did not, however, stop the workers getting poisoned, sometimes fatally. Olive Latham, who lived in Cowley with her parents in Iver Lane and worked at the factory, died from trotyl poisoning in 1916. She was 18 years old and had worked at the factory for about 5 months. Annie Perry who lived at 51 Myrtle Road, Hounslow, with her husband and two children began work there on 1st December 1915. She died of toxic poisoning at the Royal Free Hospital on 17th June 1916. In 1916 there had been 181 cases of toxic jaundice nationally, of which 52 cases were fatal. In 1917 there were 189 cases with 44 deaths. During that year, however, methods of preventing it had been found and in 1918 the figures had dramatically reduced – of 34 cases, there were only 10 deaths. A total of 4 women who worked at the Hayes factory died of the disease. During that year, however, methods of preventing it had been found and in 1918 the figures had dramatically reduced – of 34 cases, there were only 10 deaths. Despite the numbers and the scare expressed by the Press, there was no labour shortage in the filling factories. In all, from all over the country, over 300 munitions workers lost their lives as a result of TNT poisoning or explosions. In a nearby field a huge number of cylinders of acid which belonged to the Admiralty were stored. RNAS ratings were posted there in charge of the cylinders. Early in 1918, Mabel Marchant, a munition worker, was walking along a path across the field, which surrounded the factory, with three others. One of them stepped onto a cylinder of acid and another, without thinking, turned on the tap. A jet of corrosive acid struck Mabel in the face.. She was taken to hospital severely burned. She left hospital on 4th March 1918 and returned to work on 9th April 1918. Her right eyelid, face and neck were permanently disfigured. She was awarded an ex-gracia payment of £50, the Admiralty denying liability.

After a spate of accidents at Hayes and in other filling factories, by the end of 1916 Danger Building Officers were attached to each shell-filling factory. The presence of the Danger Building Officer was a guarantee that proper precautions were taken. It was not the accidents in the later months of 1916 which caused panic in the workers – it was the poisoning by TNT. As a direct result, the usual 'class' of women was by now hard to recruit which resulted in a special appeal for women of independent means. Despite the numbers of deaths and the scare expressed by the Press, there was no labour shortage in the filling factories. In all, from all over the country, over 300 munitions workers lost their lives as a result of TNT poisoning or explosions.

Scanty information was offered in both local and national newspapers concerning events which took place in munitions factories. However, it does appear that sometime in 1916, probably the explosion on about 31st March 1916 which it is known to have killed Bridget Pashon, where the girls and women were employed in filling gaines, there was a terrible explosion one morning in which several women were killed. It had been discovered that a large stock of gaines sent from America had a left-hand instead of a right-hand screw. To prevent this, the screwed-in gaines had to be stabbed in two places with a cold chisel and hammer to break the thread so that they could not unscrew. If a trace of the fulminate was ignited by the blow, the gaine would explode. Lloyd George, who was Minister of Munitions at the time, sent down a representative to visit the scene. He found one of the huts badly shattered. Inside working, still with bloodstains on the floor, he found the survivors carrying on at full speed. In May 1916 Charles Brower suffered from injuries received from timber falling off a War Office ASC motor lorry for which he received compensation. Charles Roake, a labourer at the factory, was offered £500 in respect of injuries received on 19th December 1916. He was engaged in the Traffic Department unloading 4.5inch loose shells off trucks. GWR shunters had also allowed other trucks in when a stationary truck was struck and 45 year old Mr. Roake was knocked on to the line and his arm crushed. He was taken to the doctor at the works and transferred to St. Mary's Hospital where his right arm was amputated above the elbow. In the early morning of 3rd (or 9th) January 1917, an explosion of shrapnel killed 19 year-old Thomas George Bosher of 1, Malvern Cottages, Alma Road, Windsor. On 23rd October 1917 there was a huge explosion followed by fire, which killed 28 and injured many workers. The Ministry of Munitions had already condemned the 'monkey machines', which were used for the process of 'stemming'. On the afternoon of the accident, two volunteers had been called to work on the old condemned machines. Already new screw-filling machines had been delivered to Hayes where all the work was done inside a concrete chamber, so that if there was an explosion no one would be injured. These were due to be put in place on the day after the accident. Before too long, a safety device was produced to guard workers against the dangers of explosion when stabbing gaines.

Medals were awarded for 'Devotion to duty'. Roland Basset Paine, for example, was awarded the Order of the British Empire medal for courage displayed at a severe accident which resulted in the serious mutilation of his hand. He insisted in returning to his dangerous occupation as soon as the bandages had been removed. The same medal was awarded to Violet Newton of Uxbridge.

Miss Margaret Gordon of Southall, winner of a beauty show of munition workers at Hayes in August 1917. (Gazette Newspapers)

By January 1917 women's labour supply from the London district was almost exhausted and as the workload had increased, it had become necessary to bring in workers by train. In some cases girls had arrived late at night when no lodgings were available. There were no more lodgings anywhere at Hayes. It was proposed to turn a house at Hayes into a hostel but there was local opposition, so in March 1917 five rooms at the rear of King's Hall, a Wesleyan mission at Southall, were taken over by the Ministry of Munitions. Alterations were made and it opened on 1st October 1917 for accommodating some of the women workers. Here some of the girls formed a small orchestra. Although part of the premises was used for soldiers' concerts and certain exits opened into the hostel portion, the Middlesex County Council would not allow these exits to be blocked. As the police were in short supply, the manager of the factory agreed that a Special Constable be posted at the doors to ensure the safety of the women The newly formed Women's Police Force guarded the munitions factories and would search women as they entered and departed.

In March 1917, 8,780 women and 1,849 men were employed here and in October 1918 the total stood at 8,375 women and 1,424 men. By 1918 employment at Hayes had increased four-fold and by the time hostilities were over, 78 per cent of the workers at the National Filling Factory came from the surrounding districts.

In September 1918 female Inspection Staff claimed that they were earning considerably less than the operatives of the factory whose work they supervised. An investigation was carried out when it was realised that there was serious unrest and that a strike of some, if not all of the Inspection Staff, was likely. Later that same month they were awarded an extra allowance of 3/- per week.

The total number of fuses filled were 10,000 of No. 80; 765,500 of No. 100, 5,582,800 of No. 106; 459,200 of No. 103; 1,598,500 of No. 102 and almost 8,500,000 of No. 101 – a total of 16,731,200 fuses of all types. A total of 3,864,000 friction T tubes were also filled.

A huge procession had been planned in mid October 1918 to take place on 2nd November 1918 to celebrate 'Our Day'. The Hayes Filling Factory, Cuckoo Schools in Hanwell, the Maypole and Tickler companies, the Salvation Army Band, St. Mary's

Schools and Town Band, the Fire Brigade, the Home Defence Corps, Special Constables, the Brentford Gas Company Band were amongst the huge number of participants who were going to take part. By now it was becoming clear that the terms of the Armistice were being drawn up and the war was to be coming to an end within a month or so. The plan was abandoned.

The final report of the Committee on Munitions Workers' Health noted that there had been no marked breakdown of the health of women in that industry. Evidence suggested that work before breakfast was a mistake and that Sunday labour was unpopular, uneconomical and not productive of increased output. It also stated that the great majority of workers were insusceptible to TNT and that much had been done to improve the health and increase the efficiency of the workers by the reduction in excessive drinking brought about by the Central Control Board.

By October 1918, 8,700 workers were employed in the factory and when war ended the process of the demobilisation of civilian war workers resulted in a reduction to 1,800 by January 1919 (the total number of workers at Hayes by this date had decreased by almost half - to roughly 7,000 - by far the largest decrease was at the Filling Factory) and by May 1919 there were only 700. After the war, at the storage depot in South Ruislip, there were 34 men and 2 women employed breaking down ammunition. The factory itself, apart from some of the larger sheds which were taken over by the Hayes Cocoa Company, was originally intended for use as a store at the end of the War, but became a convalescent and training centre for soldiers injured and disabled in the War.

Workshops and training places for a number of trades started, so that soldiers could see the work prior to selecting a trade. After discharge from Hayes the men were sent elsewhere for training.

In October 1919 the factory held a sale of stocks of goods acquired by the Government during the War, including 1,757 black oilskins, earthenware tumblers bearing the initials G.R., enamelled bowls and 5 tons of soap. Uxbridge UDC purchased a 20 horse-power Harding Churton Motor at a cost of £143, which was to be installed at the sewage works to drive the second 8inch centrifugal pump and also bought an automatic starting-gear. At another sale in February 1920 vast quantities of foodstuffs were sold at a 3-day public auction – lobster, sardines, corned beef, 2,500 tins of fruit and 7,000 tins of salmon. A large party of engineers and other interested parties purchased loose plant, machines, electrical equipment, tools, stores etc. The lots also included pumps, boilers, lathes, cutting machines, presses, weighing machines, 20,000 yards of electric cable, 1,000 x 2 volts NF lamps and large quantities of holders, plugs, switches, belts etc.

The National Filling Factory was put up for sale by auction on 31st March 1921. It comprised 3 large loading sheds, 5 workshops, 5 extensive assembly buildings, 63 filling sheds, 6 offices and stores, open sheds, 16 small huts, 15 clock houses and shelters, 4 magazines, 105 loading bays, water towers, 31 small brick sheds, a large timber bridge over roadway, about 7,000 feet of 6ft-8ft platform or gantry, 1300ft. of 7ft unclimbable galvanised iron fencing, about 50 water waste preventers with piping and other items. One of the tin huts was purchased by

Southall Labour Party for use as a club house, which was situated just off the Uxbridge Road.

Some industries had been ignored in the past through our inability to produce at home certain articles, this country preferring to depend on foreign counties, especially on Germany. With the shortage of material, no one could start a new business or enlarge an old one, except for war purposes. The United Kingdom Glass Company Limited opened a new factory in Dawley in late 1917 as part of an effort to develop this industry and to render this country largely independent of foreign supplies of glassware. It stood on almost 12 acres next to the Grand Junction Canal on one side and the Great Western Railway on the other. The Company acquired its own sidings. The needs of the time demanded an immediate start, so the factory starting production before the factory was complete. Boys and girls were both recruited as well as disabled soldiers. A foreman was released from the Army to train the boys in the use of the machines. It was used for the duration of War solely for manufacturing ware necessary for the Ministry of Munitions after which it was intended to lift war-time controls. The Government had decided to give every soldier at the front plum-pudding and beer at Christmas. Its first order was to make bottles to send on trucks from Hayes Station to Burton where they would be filled with beer and sent on to France in time for some Christmas cheer.

At Harlington, an unnamed inventor began a business there. He was the sole proprietor of a secret process for the recovery of steel and iron from waste metal. He supplied a high-grade of steel to munitions factories. Such work before the war had been carried out mainly by the Germans.

By the beginning of 1917 the State had gradually assumed either possession or control of railways and canals, ships and shipping, an enormous number of engineering and other works, the whole output of hay and straw etc. and in industry there was an enormous inequality of wartime demand with peacetime demand. In 1919 Government control of factories was released and normal activities were resumed.

LEISURE PURSUITS
Cinemas were patronised by both soldiers home on leave or recovering and those billeted with local families as well as those well-paid men and women who worked in the munitions and other factories. The Hayes Cinema was at one time threatened with being used as a store for war materials. Because the Botwell Brotherhood made use of the cinema in early 1915 when its new premises was being constructed, to avoid closing down it moved into its own chapel in Nield Road on 17th November 1915. Without this income, however, the cinema seems to have declined and by October 1916 had opened as a restaurant.

Public houses were the leisure-time haunts of many, including munitions workers who had more money in their pockets than they had had in pre-war times. The Government was concerned about the consumption of alcohol, particularly amongst the female munitions workers. Gypsies near Dawley Road and Keith Road were another problem locally during the middle of the war (and had to be removed as soon as possible 'in the interest of public health'), as were the wounded and recuperating Australian soldiers and some staff from the temporary military hospital situated at Southall who had been banned from Southall park for most of the war because of their bad behaviour, and very late in the war were also banned from all the public houses in Southall despite the Defence of the Realm Act forbidding the sale of intoxicants to soldiers undergoing hospital treatment. Southall Council had also imposed a 10pm curfew on them. In the Metropolitan area of Middlesex the number of convictions for drunkenness had increased from 47,000 in 1908 to 67,000 in 1914, although the number of public houses in Middlesex had been reduced by 170.The increase in drunkenness reported at the licensing session for the Brentford Division in February 1915 was thought to be caused by the growth of the population, The population in 1914 was 214,705 and in the previous year was 204,004. The Chairman in presenting his review of the past year, said that the number of cases of drunkenness dealt with at that court in 1914 was 971, as against 959 in 1913. Of that number, 776 were males and 195 females. Since the outbreak of war there had been 398 charges of drunkenness, 295 males and 103 females, and during the corresponding period of 1913 the number was 439, being 340 males and 99 females. Lloyd George began a campaign in October 1915 and the Government announced several measures which they believed would reduce the consumption of alcohol. The opening times of the pubs were reduced and in 1917 and in 1918 taxes on beers and spirits were raised to an unprecedented level.

    Within the first weeks of war, over 1,000 local footballers who were registered with the Middlesex County Football Association had joined the colours and this figure increased day by day. As young men joined up, many clubs were forced to close through lack of members. This resulted in land becoming earmarked, whilst other sports grounds had already been built upon. The MCFA cancelled all their coming season competitions and urged able-bodied men to join up without delay. As leagues and clubs disbanded local sides found opposition from various army units that were stationed nearby at Denham or Slough. All teams were encouraged to play matches to raise funds for war relief. Botwell Mission FC had joined the Hounslow and District League and after a most successful 1913-1914 season were doing just as well in wartime, but by early January 1915 however, the Hounslow League had to suspend activities. The Great Western Suburban League suspended all football fixtures for the 1914-1915 season when ten clubs dropped out – Uxbridge and Southall were the only ones remaining.

The Black Horse Public House, Hayes. (Hillingdon Local History, Archives and Museum Service)

The Uxbridge and District League had already been disbanded. Professional football was stopped in the July 1915 and replaced with regional leagues where players, who would only play on Saturdays, were unpaid. A London Works League and a Munitions League were formed for the employees of factories engaged in the war effort. Football matches were arranged between women working at local munitions factories and were held in aid of Red Cross funds. A crowd of 2,000 turned up to watch one such game at Uxbridge. The Middlesex County Football Association had hoped that cup matches would be run in the latter half of the 1918-1919 season, but this was impossible with so few clubs being in a position to resume playing.

Cricket carried on in a desultory fashion for a time as did golf. On the other hand, during the early weeks of the war and thereafter, local rifle clubs reported that membership had greatly increased, while others were formed. New rifle clubs were set up at Harmondsworth and Harlington in the early days of the war. The rifle range at Harlington was in Hatton Road. By November 1914 another club was set up in Hayes, by and primarily intended for the staff of the British Electric Transformer Co. to train themselves in home defence. Here an old cottage formed the stop butts. Electric lights were fitted both at the butts and the firing point so that practice could be carried out day or night. There was also a rifle range at Cranford. It was an outdoor range and opened for the summer season.

It took a number of years for sports clubs to recover from the war, in which some fine local players were killed in action. Frank Phillips had been one of the founders of the Old Uxbridge and Hayes United Football Club, and was also one of its prominent players. He was killed in action in France on 18th September 1918. Six members of Harlington

Cricket Club fell. Herbert Mellett, who lived at Hayes, had been captain of the Hayes and Harlington Cycling Club, which had also disbanded for the duration of war. He was with the Army Service Corps and was accidentally killed on duty at Blackdown near Aldershot, on 17th June 1915. He was 27 years old.

After the war ended, clubs made hard efforts and gradually clubs reformed, albeit sometimes years later, and were successful in reviving the pre-war activities.

TRANSPORT

Under Section 16 of the Regulation of the Forces Act 1871 the Government was given power to control all railroads. This control was to be exercised through an Executive Council composed of general managers of the railways and was set up in 1912. It consisted entirely of the general managers of the 9 leading British railway companies. Mr. Frank Potter of De Burgh Crescent, West Drayton, general manager of the Great Western Railway was one of the members of the Council. On 5th August 1914 the Government's Railway Executive Committee took over all the railways of Great Britain. All Government traffic was carried without charge and had precedence. During the fortnight of mobilisation 632 special troop trains, including 186 to bring back Territorials from their summer training camps, were run over the Great Western.

Railways became an indispensable part of the war machine not only abroad, but also at home. Ambulance trains, trains carrying soldiers and sailors on leave and then back into action, workmen's trains, and general war traffic as well as the passage of civilians placed great stress on the railway Companies. Special workmen's trains were started on the Metropolitan line. However, after the air-raids long queues formed for the workmen's trains, mostly of people who had arrived locally to escape the raiders. This exodus of people so taxed the all railways that in the spring of 1918, special restrictions on the issue of tickets were introduced. On the tubes men in uniform travelled free as they did throughout the country on trams and buses. In the end there were so many troops this also had to be withdrawn. Thousands of railway workers, many of whom were Reservists or Territorials, joined the Colours that a restraining hand had to be placed on them. By early 1915, 9358 men who were employed by the Great Western Railway were on service. Amongst those locals who enlisted was William Sargood of Hayes who had been employed as a carter by the Great Western Railway at Hayes. He was killed in action in January 1916. E. Wheeler, a labourer of the Engineering Department at Hayes, was reported to have lost his life in early 1917. Mr. M. Shadwell of Southall was a temporary creasotor at Hayes Station in the Engineering Department. He had been there for about 2 years and was killed in action in November 1914. Stanley Mott had worked in the Traffic Department at Hayes and Harlington Station. He died, possibly as a POW, on 21st September 1918, aged 24. His parents lived at Caversham.

    GWR services had already been affected when in the spring of 1915 further reductions in train services took place and Sunday services considerably curtailed. Hayes Urban District Council approached the GWR in June 1915, to provide a service of workmen's trains between Brentford and Hayes. Southall-Norwood's Clerk requested that workmen's trains be run from Brentford between 5.30 and 6am and from Southall at 6pm. They were turned down and the branch later closed down except for military use until the spring of 1920. Still further reductions to suburban and outer suburban services, affecting Uxbridge, Ealing, Windsor, Eton and Reading were made on 1st January 1916 and in July 1916 the GWR discontinued the running of certain other trains.

London buses (H.W.Wilson, The Great War)

The newly built munitions factories were turning out war material at high speed relied on any form of transport and there were not enough trains to carry the material they had made to the Front. As a result, as a matter of urgency, on 1st January 1917, ordinary passenger fares were raised by fifty per cent, restricting public travel, and large number of stations were closed, although none locally. The volume of war traffic on the GWR was swollen by the fact that there were 47 munitions works on that line, including the one at Hayes. As the war dragged on so the daily influx of workers to Hayes escalated.

During the early part of the War, many London buses, very often fitted with lorry bodies, stripped of their paint and advertisements and with windows boarded up, were amongst those sent to the front to transport troops, convey the wounded and bring up ammunition and other supplies (Parisian buses were used to transport fresh meat with great success and troop transports). Some London buses were also converted – their chassis were used for mounting anti-aircraft guns at the front. Thousands of buses plied in a regular service between the reserve troops' headquarters and the front lines in France and Flanders. They were later reinforced with wooden panels.

The number of trains required to convey the workpeople between the munitions factory at Hayes and their homes attained a maximum of 103 per day and by 1918 over 15,000 workers were daily conveyed to Hayes by special trains from up and down the line between Paddington and Windsor. The greatest number of persons conveyed on a working day was 33, 000, although 60,000 were carried in one day when the factory's sports carnival was being held. The approximate number of passengers conveyed in connection with the factory during the War was 25,000,000.

By March 1918 the Great Western Railway had carried 5,709,000 soldiers in 25,261 special troop trains. Although short of manpower, Britain's railways were able to carry a burden of traffic that grew as war progressed yet could still maintain an adequate public service right through to the end.

London buses (H.W.Wilson, The Great War)

London United Electric Tramways introduced half-fares for children in November 1914, between the hours of 8.30am and 5.30pm and up to 2pm on Saturdays. However, as reservists were called up, in November 1914 and again later, the LUET entirely withdrew certain of their services including the Sunday Nos. 89, a bus which ran between Southall and Uxbridge. Some of these buses, very often fitted with lorry bodies, stripped of their paint and advertisements and with windows boarded up, may have been amongst those sent to the front to transport troops, convey the wounded and bring up ammunition and other supplies (Parisian buses were used to transport fresh meat with great success and troop transports). Some London buses were also converted – their chassis were used for mounting anti-aircraft guns at the front. Thousands of buses plied in a regular service between the reserve troops' headquarters and the front lines in France and Flanders. Hayes Urban District Council approached the Tramway Company in July 1915, with a view to obtaining 1d workmen's fares between Hayes and Southall and Hayes and Uxbridge and the special facilities for workmen to be extended to Hayes.

There were also problems with running the buses to a correct timetable as there was a scarcity of the necessary materials to repair the trams should any fault or breakdown occur. By the end of 1915, the Company was getting short of rails for repairs and persuaded Hanwell Council to lift the unused tracks in the Lower Boston Road. The price of petrol had doubled in 1916 and when the rationing of petrol came in in 1918, travel became increasingly difficult. In October 1917 from Monday to Friday the tram service to Uxbridge was reduced and in May 1918 London United Tramways Company decided to curtail their service. As from 12th May 1918 the morning Sunday service was cancelled and on weekdays and Sundays the late night trams would run ¾ hour earlier. In mid June 1918 a full Sunday service was resumed by LUET. In early 1918 the Company had proposed a Bill to be laid before Parliament in the 1918 session for an increase in fares and to close certain portions of the route, including from the Uxbridge terminus to the Southall-Norwood boundary, as well as some other matters. They contacted all the local Councils with a vested interest. Without fail, all the local local councils were not impressed and Hayes Urban District Council joined neighbouring authorities (Uxbridge Rural District Council, Uxbridge Urban District Council, Southall-Norwood Urban District Council, and the Urban

District Councils of Ealing and Acton) to write in the most strongest of terms of their opposition to the Bill to their local MPs and petitions were lodged in the House of Lords.

GWR Train Service cancellations in February 1915 (Gazette Newspapers)

A compromise was agreed, the drafts were amended and on 21st November 1918 the Bill was passed into law. London United Tramways had been empowered under the Statutory Undertakings (Temporary) Increase of Charges Act 1918 to charge fares of 1d per mile for ordinary passengers and ½ d per mile for workmen's fares, with a minimum fare of 1d for the period of the war and for 2 years after. In mid-August an unexpected strike on a Saturday night by women workers brought trams in Uxbridge as well as the whole of West Middlesex to a standstill. Their grievance was that men had been offered a pay-rise, whereas the women had not. During the week the strike spread to the girls on the 'tube' and eventually to as far afield as Bath, Brighton, Bristol, Folkestone, Hastings and Weston-Super-Mare. Trains were packed and bikes became more commonplace. Women workers secured a 5/- per week increase.

In mid-August an unexpected strike on a Saturday night by women workers brought trams in the whole of West Middlesex to a standstill. Their grievance was that men had been offered a pay-rise, whereas the women had not. During the week the strike spread to the girls on the 'tube' and eventually to as far afield as Bath, Brighton, Bristol, Folkestone, Hastings and Weston-Super-Mare. Trains were packed and bikes became more commonplace. Women workers secured a 5/- per week increase. London United Electric Tramways also lost personnel. By December 1915, 20 LUET employees had been killed.

As the railways had come under considerable strain, road transport grew rapidly, but the more the roads were used the more they became in a bad state of disrepair. Councils carried out repairs to local roads, mainly tarring, sometimes making use of POWs, for instance in August 1918 German POWs were employed to tar the roads at Harlington. Very occasionally minor roads were also constructed, a new road from Yeading to Northolt, avoiding an awkward corner by Yeading Manor Farm, for example, was constructed in the spring of 1918. The major road repairs on roads congested with war transport were carried out in conjunction with the Military Authorities. In April 1915 the Surveyor at Hayes reported to certain requisitions he had received with regard to Yeading Lane from the Military Authorities. In June 1915, Hayes UDC approved and accepted the offer made by the Road Board for making up Yeading Lane and West End Lane – the War Department was to fund £500 and the Road

Board to lend the Council £300 for 5 years, free of interest. The work making up Yeading Lane finished at the end of July 1916. Coldharbour Lane, which had been widened in 1914, had to be repaired in early 1916 after it had been damaged during the construction of the munitions factory at Hayes. It was once again in need of repair by January 1917. In May 1917 the Borough Surveyor at Hayes received a military requisition to carry out certain repairs and widenings to West End Lane and Yeading Lane and also Coldharbour Lane and Station Road as far as the railway bridge and for the construction of a new road from Yeading Green to West End Lane at Northolt. The Surveyor was asked to submit a report on an alternative new road from Yeading Bridge to Poplar Farm and this alternative, although slightly more costly, was agreed upon. It was pointed out that should flooding occur, it would still be possible to use the old road as it was at a higher level. The Road Board offered to lend the Council £3,300 over 5 years free of interest and the War Office and Ministry of Munitions were asked to provide the balance of £4,335, which also included repairs to the existing road from Hayes to Yeading. Various owners of land, including Lord Hillingdon, Sir T. Salt and Mr. W. Lloyd Unwin, who was offered £160 per acre, were approached by the Council, which arranged for the purchase of the necessary land on the most favourable terms. In the end the cost was £7,633 and was equally divided between Hayes UDC and the Ministry of Munitions.

By the beginning of the war, the Road Board was intimating that the Middlesex County Council should construct the new Great West Road by direct labour as money was not a problem and it was urged that the road should be commenced in order to absorb the unemployed! However although the County Council took steps to purchase building material the labour required was not available and until 1919 all other operations apart from acquisitions of land were suspended. The proposed building of the Western Avenue was also deferred. Again in 1916 all Councils considered arterial road development, especially for the profitable employment of surplus labour in any period of unemployment which may arise after the War. In late 1918 the Road Board again investigated the various schemes and their reports on the suggested Western Avenue and the North Circular Road were issued as a Parliamentary Paper. It was recommended that the Western Avenue would be an almost entirely new road over 15 miles long.

Thousands of women were employed on public transport. They acted as ticket collectors, porters, ticket inspectors, booking office clerks etc. As from the early summer of 1916 a number of women were also employed as conductresses on buses and trams. These women, who wore blue uniforms, had to undergo a special course of training prior to employment.

RATIONING and the CULTIVATION OF LAND ORDER 1916

During 1915, almost a quarter of British ships had been requisitioned. With this shortage of ships, fewer goods were imported and by February 1915 various commodities had increased in price. At the end of 1916, Germany was beginning to recognise that she could not win the war on the Western Front and decided to seek victory by waging unrestricted submarine warfare in the Atlantic to starve Britain into submission. By the winter of 1916-17, German U-boats had declared unrestricted warfare on merchant ships and German submarines had sunk 632,000 tons in intensified submarine blockades. When in April 1917 one ship out of four leaving Britain's ports never returned, British shipping losses reached its peak, losing 526,000 tons - the highest loss in any month of the War, Britain's food situation became serious, almost starving Britain into defeat.

Britain imported much of the food needed for her population of around 45,000,000. This position remained secure as long as the Navy could ensure safe transit from suppliers oversees. The local paper, The Advertiser and Gazette, was amongst the first of the journals to advocate compulsory rationing.

British wheat acreage and production had declined significantly since 1861 and wheat prices fell steadily from the spring of 1915 but when supplies fell seriously short owing to a poor world harvest and following the closure of the Dardanelles, Russian wheat could not be obtained. In 1916, British wheatfields had been reduced further by a quarter of a million acres and the general production of home-grown food had fallen twelve per cent between 1915 and 1916. Not for 100 years had the price of wheat, barley and oats been so high as in early 1918. The Government had to fix prices. For the first time queues appeared at shops, but this was not on a large scale despite the influx of people to work and to shelter from air-raids.

Early in 1915, a number of local Councils got together to write to the Government imploring them to take immediate action to put a stop to the high price of foodstuffs. In the spring of 1916, again a number of local Councils wrote, in very strong terms indeed, to

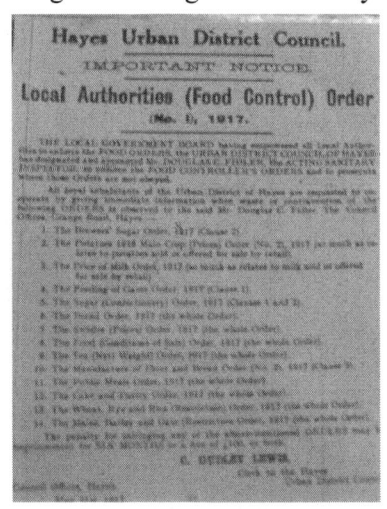

Herbert Asquith, the Prime Minister, the local MP, imploring them to take steps towards controlling the increase in the cost of food and other prime necessities. However, although controls on food had begun at an early stage in the War, by 1916 there was no real shortage of food in Britain although prices and wages had begun to rise. By 1916, however, food substitutes were used to a limited extent and by the end of that year, less food was being produced than before the war and although the convoy system cut the sinking of our ships, our food supplies were insufficient to go round at reasonable prices. The poor potato harvest of 1916 reduced the poorer people to hardship and on January 13th 1917, the first food riot occurred. The Milk Prices Order had come into force on 1917, after many Councils, including Hayes, after receiving letters from other local Councils, contacted the Local Government Board and the Prime Minister urging them to take such steps as may be necessary to control the price of milk. In 1917 despite the crisis in food supply, there was an unwillingness to bring in rationing. By this time the average working-class family needed at least an extra 15 shillings to pay for food and a further 1s 10d per week for rising fuel costs. As part of the Food for Britain Campaign, food parcels were sent out from all over Australia for distribution amongst widows.

Farmers and farmhands had been gradually called up and not much food was being produced. Further, so many people had come not only to work in the area, but refugees, billeted soldiers, wounded men in hospital etc., that there was not enough food to go round. Shopkeepers were obliged to sell their wares to everyone as it had been made illegal to only sell to regular customers and queues grew more frequent and prices rose. Queues grew more frequent and prices rose. As time went along people became anxious and appeals were made for voluntary rationing. At Uxbridge a meeting was held in February 1917 with the dual purpose of raising money for the war loan and educating the public about the necessity of voluntary rationing as outlined by Lord Rhonnda of the Local Government Board. By mid April 1917 the King, Queen and Royal Household had adopted a policy of voluntary rationing and, inspired by this, the people who followed wore a badge of purple ribbon. Lord Devonport, a rich grocer, head of Kearley and Tonge's (provision merchants) and since 1909 Chairman of the Port of London Authority and native of Uxbridge, was appointed the first Food Controller at the Ministry of Food in December 1916 and quickly put into place the restriction of the price of food and launched a voluntary rationing scheme in late May 1917.

The first national rationing scheme, applying to sugar (two-thirds of which had come from Germany and Austria-Hungary), came into force on 1st March 1917, but throughout that year local authorities introduced rationing schemes of their own. Hayes Food Control Committee, which was inaugurated in September 1917, made use of the Council Offices free of cost. Here complaints were made that certain traders were refusing to supply goods unless Sugar Cards had been deposited with them. The Council warned that in the event of such cases arising in the future proceedings would be taken. Sugar substitutes were available and some housewives resorted to using these. There was a shortage of bacon locally by the beginning of October 1917 as well as tea, bread, margarine, lard, condensed milk, rice, butter, paper and some other commodities. There was a shortage of bacon locally by the beginning of October 1917 (in the first 6 weeks of war the price of bacon rose by 10% and then remained at the same level for 8 months rising very slowly until the summer of 1917 when it rose rapidly until in February 1918 when it was 140% above the pre-war level) as well as tea, bread (the price of which had risen to 11½d by September 1917), margarine, the home production of which, because of the difficulties of transportation, had gone up by 20% in the years between 1913 and 1918, and which compensated for the deficiency of the butter supply, lard, condensed milk, rice, butter (since 1913 either unobtainable or at a prohibitive cost partly due to the great diminution of imports, in some way caused by the Maypole Dairy Company at Southall who were unable to import Danish butter from their buying stations in Denmark), paper and some other commodities. Prices rose.

By 1918 the food situation was at its most serious. Local Food Committees were set up – the one at Hayes in late 1917. In the spring of 1918 the country had only two weeks' supply of food left. Even hospitals and schools suffered. They had considerable difficulty obtaining supplies, food, as well as drugs which were also in short supply, putting up prices, and food rationing applied to patients and staff alike.

The compulsory rationing of certain foods - meat and bacon, butter and margarine (from the end of 1917 local bakers were already using cocoa-butter as an indifferent substitute to margarine), came into operation in the last week of February 1918 and affected London and Middlesex, Hertfordshire, Essex, Kent and Surrey. Early in April the rest of the country was also rationed. Food was distributed almost equally between the rich and the poor more than ever before. Customers were allotted to particular retailers who would be supplied by a specific wholesaler. Each household was issued with two ration cards, one for butcher's meat and bacon and the other for butter or margarine. Uxbridge butchers announced that they would only supply their regular customers on production of sugar cards and on at least one occasion when these butchers received unexpectedly high amounts of meat, they opened on Sunday. Butchers were expected to give preference to unsatisfied demands from the previous week. Queues all but disappeared. However, there were various summonses for people selling products at too high a price. It was commonly thought that wartime shortages of food would lead to illnesses and possibly also to early deaths in certain civilian communities.

Rationing was not only confined to food. Coal, which by early 1915 had risen in price by 20%, was another necessary commodity of which there was a shortage in Greater London during the winter of 1916-17, and queues of people, in which children predominated, besieged the coal dealers. The Filling Factory used only a small supply of coal and coke and bought them locally under the Price of Coal (Limitation) Act of 1915. Coal rationing was introduced in London in the summer of 1917 and was extended to the rest of the country a year later – the Household Fuel and Lighting Order. The Order applied to all consumers of coal, coke or other fuel for heating, cooking or purposes other than industrial. A Coal Overseer was appointed. Wasting cinders was a punishable offence! One way of saving coal was put forward – to fill drainpipes with 1 part cement to 9 parts coal dust, ramming this mixture down and adding water. It was supposed to burn for hours. Church services were confined to daylight hours followed by theatres, cinemas, music halls and restaurants. In the summer of 1916 the Daylight Saving, or Summer Time, came into effect which enabled industries to make fuel savings. Restrictions on petrol were imposed early in the war and became more tightened as hostilities progressed.

By 1916 the cost of paper had almost trebled. On February 14th 1916 the Middlesex Education Committee wrote to all the managers of Council and Non-Provided schools the following letter:- *'In view of the great increase in the price of paper and of the great difficulty which will be experienced in obtaining paper, I am directed by my Committee to ask you to be good enough to instruct your Head Teachers to be as economical as possible when ordering exercise books, drawing books, examination paper etc., and as far as possible to commence using slates in stock at once...'* Instructions were also issued that both sides of the paper were also to be used. School magazines either ceased altogether or became much smaller.

By mid 1917 Parish magazines were printed on inferior paper and were reduced in length whilst costing more. In January 1918, because of the enormous increase in the price of raw materials, the local paper increased its cost by ½d to 2d. Parish magazines also became more expensive. National newspapers, which were under Government censorship and monitored to ensure they maintained morale, were in 1918 reduced to 4 pages. Sunday papers had stopped being published by this time. The Uxbridge Gazette had also reduced in size to save paper and already by early 1916 could only be obtained by regular order. In late 1917 or early 1918, the Gazette was one of the first local papers in the country to organise a house-to-house collection of waste paper. Before the end of 1917, perhaps even in 1916, John King's Waste Paper Depot was opened in the High Street at Uxbridge where waste paper was bought. In the spring of 1918 local milkmen were asking for their payments as they no longer had the paper to write the bills. At about the same time, tickets used on the LUET route from Uxbridge to Shepherds Bush were in fact those for use between Raynes Park and Kingston.

The 'Evening News' in mid August 1914 had carried advice on the vegetables to plant for food supply to those who had gardens or plots of land. This advice came from Royal Horticultural Society and was also printed in the local paper. The importance of producing food for others was stressed. Before 1916 allotments were virtually unknown, although there had been much demand for allotments in Pinkwell Lane, Harlington, when they were laid out in 1912. But by Christmas 1916 the allotment campaign was well under way, spurred on by the gravity of the food situation. The Government issued a Cultivation of Lands Order facilitating the acquisition of land for smallholdings and market gardens in January 1917. With this Order, Parish Councils and Urban District Councils scheduled land for cultivation after touring the locality. It was thought that some land would be suitable for farmers, for allotments or as grazing land although sometimes it meant that new fencing would be needed which was not available. War Agricultural Committees were set up in each area and a parallel, the Board of Agriculture, set up similar committees in each of the boroughs of the country. They were free to choose their own titles and were formed by and under the authority of the Borough Councils and UDCs. Hayes Food Control Committee set up a War Agricultural Committee in the district in November 1917. Private gardens were also turned over to vegetable growing. Allotment patrols were organised and growers took turns to guard their own and neighbour's plots.

Already in December 1916 the Great Western Railway had offered their staff tenancies of ground alongside the railway at the annual rent of 3d or 4d per perch according to the locality and in the *'case of any tenancies arranged not later than 25th March next, the land will be granted RENT FREE for the next two years should it not have been previously cultivated.'*

The Gramophone Company, almost as soon as war broke out, began cultivating the whole of their waste ground and employed 8 more men to carry out the work. The boys from the Jewish School were also cultivating two acres of land at Hayes. At the beginning of 1917, Mr. W. Chick offered to let that portion of his uncultivated land in Drayton Road to persons who had applied to the Council for land to cultivate. In April 1917, an instructor and some boys from the School offered to dig any allotments that belonged to men serving in HM forces. The local Council accepted this offer. In April 1917, Mr. Shackle offered to let about one acre of his land near Printing House Lane for allotments for 2 years ending 25th March 1919 when the land would be put up for sale for building purposes. These 10 pole allotments were at a rate of 4/- per plot for the first year and 5/- per plot for the second. Rosedale Field was obtained for war allotments in February 1918 on the understanding that it would be surrendered of required for building purposes. However, by mid 1918 there was disquiet when other Councils noticed that some surplus land at Hayes was not let for allotments, but for 'other purposes'. At Harlington by the spring of 1917 a piece of ground in Redmead Road was being used as allotments. In mid February 1918 a meeting was held at the Hambro Hall, Dawley Road to discuss forming an Allotment Holders Society at Hayes, which was set up later that year as the Hayes and Harlington Allotment Association. By April 1918 waste ground opposite the Police Station had been turned into allotments and girl workers at the National Filling Factory were cultivating food crops for their own consumption on spare ground at the works and, for those using St. George's Hall, on land at Southall. By August 1918 the factory was almost self-sufficient. Not only had they a prosperous vegetable farm running at the Works, but also a successful piggery, rabbitry and a poultry farm. They also breed cattle.

The Southern Federation of Allotment Holders affiliated to the National Union of Allotment Holders covered the area of London and Southern Counties. It was reported in February 1918 that membership in the last month had increased by almost 5,000 to 15, 000 and by the end of hostilities exceeded 40, 000. The demand for houses was so great that in 1920 some allotment holders from all around the Borough were notified that their plots would be required for building purposes and, therefore, their renting the ground would cease.

As the war went on more and more women were required to fill the gaps caused by men going off to war. In February 1916 there was a call for 400,000 women to carry on agricultural work previously carried out by the men who were now being called up for duty. In the summer of 1916 the Minister of Agriculture foresaw a serious shortage of horticultural labour. In January 1917 when a new Minister took office the Women's Land Army was born, funded by the Government. The Land Army was divided into 3 sections-agricultural, timber cutting and forage (for army horses). Women signed on for either 6 months or a year. If an application was successful the Government offered an initial wage of 20s a week and a free uniform. After passing an efficiency test the wage was raised by 2s a week. Women were expected to go to whichever part of the country the Selection Board thought most fit. Various training schemes were set up in different parts of the country. They wore 'uniforms' of khaki knickers with puttees, long coats and 'wide-awake' hats. They started work at 6a.m. and, with intervals for breakfast and dinner, worked until 5.30p.m. A cottage on the estate was placed at their disposal where they did their own housekeeping. At a meeting held at Lady Hillingdon's residence a District Committee of the Middlesex Women's Agricultural Committee was formed. Many women also worked as plough teams. On 21st August

1917, the Corn Production Act 1917 was passed. It provided for the fixing of minimum rates of wages applicable to everyone employed in agriculture, including work on farms, market gardens, orchards, nursery grounds, woodlands and osier land. By the end of the War there were about 250,000 'land girls'. In 1919 the local paper reported that over 5000 women in the Land Army wished to remain in agriculture.

Many local residents took to keeping pigs and poultry. Some Councils, however, considered the keeping of swine a nuisance and passed Byelaws in 1914 to abate the problem. George Salter of 'Syringa', Cromwell Road had been keeping pigs for some time and in June 1916, at Hayes, the Council were alerted that he was keeping a pig contrary to by-laws regulating the keeping of pigs within the Urban District. In September 1915 he was given 8 weeks notice to remove his swine and litter. However, by the beginning of 1916 he still had his pigs. He had not been able to get rid of them he informed the Council, because of an outbreak of swine fever. New by-laws came into force in mid 1916. Mr. Salter was given notice that he was to liable to face prosecution under the new Order. After a lengthy dispute, in late November 1916 Mr. Salter gave an undertaking in writing to remove his pigs and refrain in future from contravening the by-laws. He still had the pigs in February 1917 but had applied to the Council the previous month to keep them and had been turned down. However, in February 1917 the Board of Agriculture issued a communication with respect to the steps to be taken to increase the number of pigs. In March 1917, the Council realising there was a vital necessity to encourage householders to increase all livestock for the benefit of human consumption, rescinded their previous notice and allowed him, and others, to keep swine and pig clubs started to be formed all over the district.

The Uxbridge and District Bee Keeping Association noticed a lively interest in the study when eight new members were voted to the Society in March 1918. In March 1918 the Harmondsworth and Harlington Sparrow, Starling and Rat Club was formed with the object of decreasing the grain-eating pests. Between 1st March and 1st September 1918, the following numbers were brought to the headquarters and paid at the following rates: rats 2s a dozen, 655; sparrows at 3d a dozen, 586; sparrow eggs at 2d a dozen, 308; starlings at 4d a dozen, 33 and starlings' eggs at 3d a dozen, 15. As from the new season commencing October 5th 1918 it was proposed to pay for mice at the rate of 3d per dozen.

When war ended the bug for allotments had taken hold and in common with the Second World War, rationing continued long after the conclusion of hostilities and was not fully abolished until 3 years after the war ended.

FUND RAISING and COMFORTS

From the moment war was declared, funds for this and that were started, far too many to mention here. Even before the National Relief Fund was developed, a Relief Fund was opened for Middlesex, which was divided into districts with local sub-committees. The National Relief Fund Committee No. 12, covered Hayes, Harlington and Cranford. These committees were given the power to act at once. Relief measures were also quickly set up and dealt with the local effects of the war, including to ensure food supplies and to co-ordinate other aspects of the war effort including the care of the wounded at home. Local funds were opened. Eventually local Relief Funds amalgamated into the National Relief Fund, which had been inaugurated by the Prince of Wales and aimed to centralise the work. However, by and large, the anticipated levels of distress were not realised and much of the sums raised went to other causes, mainly the Red Cross.

In order to reduce borrowing and raise funds for the war effort, the Government produced certificates, stamps and posters, sold to the public through a variety of outlets. This is one stamp from the series 'The war in the air'.

Work quickly got under way to raise money for good causes, knit and sew garments for the poor or for the troops, sew bandages for the wounded, prepare parcels for Prisoners of War etc. Working parties were set up all over the place, flag days sprung up for various causes and funds were started to raise money for some or other purpose. Girls knitted socks, mittens, mufflers and helmets for the troops. The Middlesex Cinema War Fund was also set up in September 1914 for the relief of widows and children of Middlesex soldiers and sailors killed in action.

In the months of September and October 1914, when only a relatively small percentage of men were registered as unemployed, the percentage of women standing idle was three times as great. Queen Mary stepped in and inaugurated the Queen's 'Work for Women Funds' for women who wanted to work rather than receive charity. A grant was made out of the National Relief Fund. The money had come from a response to that appeal and was paid into the National Relief Fund for the sole purpose of the various projects and relief purposes for women. Over 300 branches were established throughout the country. Comforts for the troops, clothing, blankets, respirators etc were all made and money was collected.

The Queen had formed Queen Mary's Needlework Guild in 1914 and voluntary needlewomen mobilised themselves everywhere. War Hospital Supply Depots were formed at Battersea, Blackheath, Hampstead, Market Harborough, Plymouth, Streatham and Wimbledon, branches of St. Marylebone (the Central Depot Surgical Branch of Queen Mary's Needlework Guild). Work guilds were formed in connection with the central depot, at Uxbridge and at Iver Heath, to make bandages or dressings of any kind by hand. There was a guild branch at Harlington and one covering the areas of Harmondsworth, Sipson, Longford and Heathrow. The voluntary workers, each week subscribed to the running expenses of their depot and the whole of the sums coming in from the public were solely devoted to the purchase of material. Girls in Hillingdon, through the help of Lady Hillingdon, distributed knitted garments including 'comforts' - socks, mufflers, gloves and mittens - to various places for those on active service and scrap-books for local and London hospitals. Lady Hillingdon, who worked assiduously on behalf of the Guild with many willing workers in the parishes of Hillingdon, Cowley, Hayes, Harlington, Harmondsworth, Uxbridge and other districts, in February 1915 reported that she had forwarded more than 3000 articles to Queen Mary's Needlework Guild and 517 articles to the London Needlework Guild since War had been declared. All went to soldiers and sailors. Many sewing parties of voluntary workers also engaged in making shirts and other garments for troops sprang up all over England and did valuable work.

In celebration of Queen Mary's birthday in 1917 (28th May), many branches of QMNG in the UK and Canada sent a 'shower of gifts' for the soldiers and sailors. *Over 100,000 gifts were received of all kinds –games, pipes, walking sticks, writing material, blankets etc* (WILSON, The Great War)

War Savings Associations were set up under the National War Savings Committee. Children purchasing War Savings Stamps or subscribing through a War Savings Association, or adults purchasing on behalf of a child, were issued with pictured stamps on demand – one for each 6d spent. The Government spent money on all kinds of things from paying for the war and the reconstruction of housing schemes, health reforms and education after the war as well as for arranging for finding work for demobilised men. The Government continuously borrowed money at short notice by means of Treasury Bills and in order to repay them money was required which could only be obtained by all the citizens of the

State continuing to purchase War Savings Certificates and War Bonds.

A special War Committee launched the YMCA Huts Fund in November 1914, to provide dining halls and recreation rooms for munitions factories and servicemen and sleeping accommodation, amongst other things. It was a nationwide appeal for £25,000 but later increased by another £25,000. In the first two years of war the subscriptions amounted to £830,000. Women from the Hayes Filling Factory through force of circumstances ate their midday meals under the canopy of heaven. A temporary centre in Hayes Station Wesleyan Schoolroom had opened for them in April 1916 but proved within the first two days to be insufficient. A YWCA hut was erected in Keith Road, Hayes, in September 1916 for the local munitions workers and almost a year later permission was given for part of the temporary premises to be used for sleeping accommodation for the period of the War.

In December 1914 Mrs. Roberts of The Firs, Hayes End, thought of a scheme whereby baskets were placed at various shops and stores and people were invited to put parcels into them for wounded soldiers. She appealed for residents in the districts of Cowley, Iver, Iver Heath and Gerrards Cross to associate with the work by undertaking to use their places as depots. This scheme was taken up by the Daily Mail and proved to be an enormous success. By Christmas, eight hospitals had received parcels and another consignment had been sent as a New Year's gift to King's College Hospital. This scheme was probably carried out until 1918. In 1915 Mr. J. Newman of Harlington appealed for new-laid eggs to send to the National Egg Collection.

The absence from home of men on Military Service in many instances left their wives or mothers in a state of economic instability until their separation allowance from the Military Authorities arrived. The children could not be fed. On 7th August 1914, the Education (Provision of Meals) Act became law. It gave a local Education Authority, without any application to the Board of Education, to spend out of the rates such sums as may be necessary to meet the cost of food for children attending public elementary schools within their area on both days when the school meets and on other days. There was a larger amount of distress than at any time in any previous year since free meals were given by the Education Authorities. Very few children whose fathers had enlisted were being fed, although it wasn't usually long before the mother received the separation allowance.

Local offices of The Soldiers' and Sailors' Families Association (SSFA), which for many years had alleviated the difficulties arising where the breadwinner had gone off to war, were started with voluntary staff. Their biggest work was visits and the advancing of money to distressed families until the separation allowance came in. They only dealt with NCOs and men. By the end of 1914 Lady Hillingdon was president for Middlesex, as she had been during the Boer War, with Dr. Christopher Addison of Northwood as vice-president and the Rev. Prebend C.M. Harvey, vicar of Hillingdon, treasurer. The Uxbridge Division of Middlesex covered the whole of the modern London Borough of Hillingdon and included Cranford and Northolt. In the first year or so of the war, 54 cases of hardship were dealt with at Hayes and 25 from Harlington. In the same period, 14 families from Cranford received assistance. In late 1914, the SSFA offered to pay two weeks arrears of rent on 12 Rosedale Avenue, the home of Mr. J. Edwards, and to contribute 2/- weekly towards the rent in future. War Pensions Committees were also set up.

A National Egg Collection for the Wounded Committee in 1915 appealed to the local Community to help towards supplying new-laid eggs for the wounded soldiers and sailors. The movement had the approval of the War Office and was a great success.

The 'Gazette' started a fund for supplying Middlesex 'Tommies' at the front with cigarettes, almost a soon as the broke out. Various other funds were also set up including those for soldiers and sailors, Prisoners of War and Belgian refugees.

Of the schools, the boys of the Jewish School at Hayes grew food in the summer for serving men. Dawley Infants' School sold patriotic flags in June 1915 and gave 10/- to the Harlington branch of the QMNS and later collected 14/- for the Jack Cornwall ward at Richmond.

<u>DEFENCE</u>

Immediately after War had been declared, precautionary protective measures were taken by arrangement with the military authorities and taken in hand by the railway companies. The Police, Boy Scouts, Cadet Corps and others were also called upon to guard the railways, although no unarmed watchman could serve on lines of primary importance. Our network of railways constituted indispensable lines of communications for troops, supplies, guns, ammunition, conveyance of the wounded, the supply of foodstuffs etc. There was also a possible threat from enemy aliens who might amass information as to the vulnerable points - bridges, viaducts, tunnels etc. Therefore precautionary measures to protect them from attack and interruption had to be taken. At first policemen guarded all railway bridges in the district day and night. Gradually Regulars or Territorials began guarding local stations, bridges and tunnels. The 4th King's Own Territorials guarded the GWR railway at Hayes where in the early days of the war, the Gramophone Company lent a gramophone to help the troops guarding the line there to pass the time pleasantly. In October 1914 Private Thomas Betts of Barrow-in-Furness, one of the Territorials engaged in guarding the railway bridges at Southall, was accidentally shot dead by Private Clucas to whom he was talking. After some time, Clucas thought he had heard someone approaching. He turned round sharply in order to challenge, his rifle went off and the charge entered Bett's head. This and other similar although not always so tragic circumstances, led the Territorials to be withdrawn in November and replaced by National Guards from Devon.

Local Volunteer Forces, affiliated to the National Voluntary Reserve were begun and Local Volunteer Training Corps (VTCs), allied to the Central Association of Voluntary Training Corps, were formed to help protect the country from possible invasion. They were composed of men not eligible for the Regular or Territorial Army for various reasons and were expected to encourage recruiting and undertake a certain amount of military training. The men were expected to remain in the Corps for the duration of the war. Voluntary contributions and subscriptions met expenses. Official khaki was issued to those who passed a test of comparative fitness.

They were armed with Lee-Enfield rifles and issued with a Lewis machine gun for instruction purposes. There was a final examination on the Lewis gun at the Wellington Barracks. Defence guards were undertaken by the Uxbridge Corps at various establishments including the Hayes Filling Factory and the Dump at South Ruislip. Several of its members also undertook three months service on the east coast defences.

Soldiers guarding Bourne Bridge – a railway bridge near EMI. (Hillingdon Local Studies, Archives and Museum Service)

In April 1916, National Guards and the Royal Defence Corps were created, mainly old soldiers invalided from the fighting fronts. The Royal Defence Corps was later known as the National Reservists.

Much of the bombing of Britain was indiscriminate, although military targets were in most cases sought. Usually the bombing was sporadic with only the occasional sustained bombing. Nevertheless there were a considerable number of casualties and heavy material damage. Although fewer bombs were dropped by aeroplanes than by airships, more casualties and damage were caused by them. This was probably because attacks by aeroplanes were directed towards cities and towns, whereas airships dropped many bombs indiscriminately from great heights – and often in open country in order to lighten airships.

By August 1914 only 30 Anti-Aircraft (AA) guns were deployed in the United Kingdom, and 25 of these were 1-pounder 'pom-poms' – remnants from the Boer War. In London there was an old 'pom pom' and a naval 6-pounder, very clumsily mounted. At the end of October 1914 the Royal Artillery were placed in charge of defending everywhere but the capital and the Admiralty was confirmed in the responsibility for the defence of London – aeroplanes, guns and searchlights, temporarily assisted by four Royal Flying Corps aircraft from Joyce Green at Dartford and Hounslow, two at each, of other large undefended towns and for dealing with enemy aircraft crossing the coast. Military airships also guarded London.

After an airship raid on London, the city's first, on the night of 31St May/1st June 1915 killing seven people, other 3-inch guns increased London defences to eight. Until 1917 there were only 16 guns, comprised of AA Defence Force fixed gun and searchlight positions, the Royal Naval Anti-Aircraft Mobile Brigade with, eventually, 14 guns mounted on lorries and another mobile force equipped only with light AA guns, defending London, mostly manned by Royal National Volunteer Reservists (RNVR) part-timers. It was probably at this time that a searchlight was situated near the Uxbridge Road and east of Yeading Lane.

The deficiency in these defences was emphasised by the raids of September 1915. On 1st October 1915 orders were issued by the Admiralty for guns, searchlights and aeroplanes to be brought to

London as a precautionary measure against aerial attacks.

Part of London's Western Sub-Command showing the positions of the Guns and Searchlights (RAWLINSON, The Defence of London)

By February 1916 the total number of guns in the London district amounted to 65. Two Anti-Aircraft guns had been mounted in a field adjoining the Hayes Filling Factory but these caused a great deal of concern and a request was made to move them at least a mile away. Aeroplane searchlights were situated at Harmondsworth, Uxbridge and Eastcote and manned in the first instance by Special Constables.

In September 1916, the country was divided into two AA Defence Zones. The 'Ever Ready Zone', where all defences were in permanently readiness for action covered this area. In April 1917 this Zone was divided and renamed as Zones 'X' and 'Y', and in May 1917, the Army took control of all defences and a 'London Air Defence Area' was created. Rings of defences surrounded the Capital with guns in the central area with an inner ring of AA guns at about a 5 mile radius. A cordon of thirteen-pounder mobile Anti-Aircraft guns and searchlights around the north-western fringes of London surrounded this area where fighter aircraft could patrol. Beyond this arc was a circle of gun defences surrounding the Home Counties, with outlying gun areas in Kent and Essex.

Outside this circle was another searchlight ring. London had balloon aprons each consisting of three Caquot captive balloons 500 yards apart and connected by horizontal wire from which was suspended at 25 feet intervals, steel wires 1,000 feet in length. Eventually the height was raised to around 10,000 feet. This forced the raiders to keep above that height and so enable the defending machines the more easily to hunt them. Gun defence Sub-Commands were formed and from 1917 to 1918, London's Western Sub-Command, which covered this area, consisted of 19 gun stations with twelve fixed 75mm French guns on mounts, four 'mobile' 75mm French auto-canons and three 3-inch calibre British anti-aircraft guns and 36 searchlight stations, which extended from about 2 miles beyond Watford to 3 miles south of Bromley and from Windsor to Grove Park. The Sub-Command HQ was established in the Metropolitan Waterworks at Putney Heath. Each gun-station was under the charge of an officer and manned by a sergeant, a corporal and between 16 and 18 men. There were double crews at each station in order that the crews could work on alternate nights. Central stations (such as Hyde Park, Paddington Recreation Ground, Parliament Hill and Deptford) remained in the charge of the RNVR. Beyond them was a ring of inner guns, such as Richmond, Hounslow, Hanwell, Acton, Horsenden Hill and Kenton, with an outer ring extending through Eastcote, Windsor, Staines, Hampton, Morden, Croydon and Bromley to Grove Park.

The searchlight stations were manned by a non-commissioned officer with from 6 to 8 men, according to the various types of engines by which the electric current was supplied to the searchlight.

Around London a circle of searchlights was gradually drawn so that close to the end of the war there were over 200, many of immense power. Most gun-stations were served by two searchlights, which were known as 'fighting lights'. The Eastcote Light served the Horsenden Hill gun and the Uxbridge Common and Wood End Lights served the gun at Hanwell. Searchlights at West Drayton and Langley served the Hayes gun, believed to have been situated at Dawley between the railway line and the Grand Union Canal.

An elaborate telephone system was adopted so that the searchlight stations could communicate with gun-stations to which they were attached and the gun-stations could then communicate with HQ. Each gun-station was also connected to at least two Observation Posts, which were situated in opposite directions and some way away from the guns in order to observe the bursts of the shells and to advise the gun as to the position of the bursts in relation to the target. The Observation Posts for the Hayes gun were at Cowley Peachey (or Hillingdon) and at Southall, and the O.P. for the Hounslow gun was situated in or near Cranford Park. The guns were of various types, as were the searchlights. Each gun and searchlight station was provided with a table fixed in the open in the immediate vicinity of the gun or light. On this was a map of the immediate district. It was covered with glass and illuminated from underneath. All information reaching a station was at once carried to the table and the position of an advancing target established on the squared map. As soon as the target was definitely located from any station, the station immediately reported the fact, and also the squares through which the target was passing at that moment together with other information such as speed, altitude and direction. These OP's became of considerable value as sources of information during raids. The police up to a 60-mile radius were instructed to warn the city on the approach of enemy aircraft.

To deal with airships which evaded fixed guns, mobile defence was quickly improvised by the Anti-Aircraft Corps. Machine guns with high-angle mountings were installed on motor chassis together with searchlights. A number of London United Tramways vehicles, including some operating on the Uxbridge Road route, were modified to carry 60cm searchlights, guns and their crew. One of their observation action stations was outside the Jewish Boys' School at Hayes. Their sole purpose was for night time use during the Zeppelin raids. They were painted dark green and had their lower deck windows boarded up. All numbers and letters were obliterated and painted in white along the inside of the dash was a War Office number. Much of the lower deck housed the generator, the rest of the space was used as a mess.

In the summer of 1917, 90 Fire Brigades in an area of 750 square miles were organised to give aid in London in any emergency. All Reservists were called up from the front and engineer detachments attached to the firemen were doubled. When the first air-raid warning reached the Fire Brigade its supports closed in from the outlying area towards the most dangerous points.

The defence of London never did reach its intended potential, unlike Paris which, after a raid on January 29th 1916 which killed 26 people, thereafter developed its defences so well that the French capital was left unassailed by Zeppelins.

POLICE

The existing police forces of the country, which had largely recruited men discharged from the fighting services, had suddenly been deprived of the services of all their Reservists, both Army and Navy. Not only was the strength of the regular constabulary reduced and efforts were made to spread their work amongst those of their colleagues left behind, but the duties devolved to the Police during wartime became more numerous and varied as we have seen. In the Metropolitan area, all police leave was cancelled for the first year.

Colonel Sir Edward Ward, Bart, Permanent Under-Secretary of State, War Office, 1901-1914, inspecting the 'X' Division of the Special Police at Blackheath (H.W. Wilson, The Great War)

As it was at the time of the Boer War, it was these types of men, those above military age, those in some essential occupation and men physically unfit for war services who were encouraged to volunteer as Special Constables, an amateur service created by the War. This new service sprang into action at the outbreak of war and all strata of society turned up in their numbers to enlist. By 24th August 1914, 20,000 men and by the end of 1914, 31,000 men had enrolled and were given the same powers, duties and privileges as a regular policeman. They had to take the King's Oath and were issued with a constable's warrant and a whistle. At first they wore a blue and white armlet and some months later were issued with a blue uniform cap. A uniform came later still but only after a certain number of drills and duty 'turns' had been completed.

A Special Constabulary Force for the whole of the London Metropolitan Police district, an area which embraced all the environs of London and all London itself apart from the City was amongst the very first to be established. There were 21 divisions in the Metropolitan Police district of which most of the local area formed 'X' division, although it appears that Cranford and Harlington were in 'T' Division, as Hayes had been at some time. Enrolment began in Uxbridge Petty Sessional Court and Northwood Police Station in the second week of August 1914. 33 members from the parishes of Hillingdon West, Ruislip, Yiewsley, West Drayton, Uxbridge, Hayes and Hillingdon East, were enrolled. They began their monotonous duties later on that month and undertook night duties at vulnerable positions, for example the Uxbridge Gas Works, observation posts, etc.

Each Metropolitan Police Division had its own motor-transport section and a fleet of London buses was given to the Metropolitan Police force to facilitate the transport of police between divisions when the need arose. A third of the number was always on duty and available for service. Thus, at a moment's notice, at a call for police into any of the London divisions, a hundred or more buses, if need be, could set off without delay to bring in police from other divisions. On Saturday 7th July 1917 when a fleet of nearly 30 German aeroplanes flying in duck formation raided London, Special Police in their hundreds were collected from the division and despatched to East London, where the damage was the greatest. During and after air-raids in October 1917 they were provided with steel helmets to protect them from the hail of steel fragments scattered by anti-aircraft guns.

During air-raids the Special Constabulary was always on duty – occasionally for 5-6 hours at a stretch. Over 100 calls were sometimes received in the night-time. From the beginning of 1915, the 'Specials' at Hayes had a vantage point on top of the Gramophone Works. During the air-raids the police would have hardly coped but for the Specials who were helping patrol the streets for any signs of light, manning the observation posts, arranging the 'take cover' notices etc. As time went on, the duties of the 'Specials' changed considerably and they became efficient and available in first-aid work. In 1916 it was the Special Constabulary in one of their vehicles who transported the traitor, Roger Casement, across London to Brixton Prison. By August 1917, London's Special Constables had taken over from the military people the manning of observation posts.

On 30th April 1916, Divisions of Special Constables from all parts of London attended the Albert Hall for a giant Church parade. 'X' Division met at Westbourne Park and travelled to the Albert Hall via Victoria Gate and Alexandra Gate to

Exhibition Road. Headed by the band of the Middlesex Regiment they marched across Hyde Park to the Hall. The whole of the divisions in the Metropolitan Police area – a total of about 20,000 – mustered at four different centres of London and a special service was conducted in each of the four districts. In May 1918, more than 7,000 Special Constables paraded at Regent's Park to receive the Silver Star awarded to all Specials who had enrolled prior to January 1915 and had served continually since.

Growing industrial unrest in July 1918 caused widespread strikes. In August 1918 there was a strike of 11,000 London tram and bus workers for more pay for women workers. So suddenly and unexpected, on the night of August 30th about 14,000 Metropolitan Police stopped work for an increase in pay, including their war bonus, and for their union to be officially recognised. Not a single policeman was on beat duty and only a handful was out controlling traffic. The 'Specials' had been called out, but according to common report the response was rather half-hearted. Although this strike went on for nearly 3 days there was no increase in the crime levels. Their demands for more pay were met.

The Armistice was signed on 11th November 1918 and the duties of the Special Police ceased on 23rd November 1918. However, in March 1919 'X' Division was called upon to provide Special Constables for special duty in London at the funeral of Nurse Edith Cavell. She had been shot as a spy by the Germans at the beginning of August 1915 and buried where she fell. On March 17th 1919, her body was exhumed and brought back to England for reburial at Norwich Cathedral.

In early October 1921, the Duke of York presented long-service medals to members of the Metropolitan Special Constabulary at Hyde Park. Every man who served in the war force and put in at least 150 duties, was entitled to the medal. Service in the then present reserve also counted, but it had to be three times the length of that required in the war force. 5,500 officers and men from 24 police divisions took part. All the chief officers of 'X' Division were present. The Ruislip section and the Hayes section (under Sergeant Gardner) paraded with the Uxbridge section, prior to the medal presentation. After an inspection, the Duke of York handed medals to staff, divisional and senior station officers. At the same time commandants handed medals at tables near by to the inspectors and sub-inspectors who in turn distributed them to the men on parade.

BOY SCOUTS and GIRL GUIDES

Some Scout groups had folded prior to hostilities breaking out, but the Scout and Guide movements had great appeal during World War One and were active throughout the war. Most of the local Scoutmasters were called to active service with the Territorials on 19th August 1914. They were under the personal direction of the District Commissioner. Each scoutmaster was instructed to prepare lists of scouts willing to mobilize for action. The local police received a copy of these lists. A general circular from the Chief Scout described the possible duties of the Scouts volunteering for service. Their duties were not of a military nature but of a material service to the country – communications, guarding bridges and other vulnerable places, collecting information on transport, acting as guides and orderlies, forwarding dispatches dropped by aircraft, etc. Sea Scouts were to watch estuaries and ports, guide vessels in unbuoyed channels, showing lights to friendly vessels etc. The local Scouts were placed at the disposal of the police and the Council Relief Committee and those on Government or special duty would be on a ration allowance. A shilling a day was allowed to each officer and Scout employed, but District Commissioners were requested to keep the expenses down where possible as the headquarters fund was limited. Each Scout in uniform also had to wear the fleur de lys buttonhole badge. This was mandatory in order to be recognized as members of the association.

LUET tram on the Uxbridge Road at Hayes
(Hillingdon Local Studies, Archives and Museum Service)

The Scout and Guide movements had great appeal during World War One. Scouts were active throughout the war. Within the first few hours after war was declared the Scouts had taken up the duty of guarding important railway bridges, water-works and telegraph and cable lines throughout the country – day and night. The Army and the Territorial troops later relieved them. They patrolled cliffs with coastguards and provided a messenger service for the police, stood guard over strategic bridges and telephone lines and had bugles to alert the public sheltering from Zeppelins and aircraft that all was now clear. Scouts who carried out war service of one kind or another were awarded a little strip of red material with a yellow date on it, which was worn on the right breast.

Scouts at Hayes were taught rudimentary skills in fire-brigade work in early 1918. Guides carried out tasks such as helping out in canteens, hospitals acted as stretcher-bearers and first-aiders. They also entertained. Scouts were also to collect specific items such as jam jars, tin cans, string and cotton waste. In August 1918, the National Salvage Corps wrote to councils as to the importance of the collection of fruit stones and nutshells for war purposes. The Surveyor at Uxbridge was instructed to write to the heads of all local schools and Boy Scouts in the district asking them to organise the collection of these. Scouts who carried out War service of one kind or another were awarded a little strip of red with a yellow date on it, which was worn on the right breast.

The pupils from the Parisian school for English young ladies at Drayton Hall in 1915 formed a private officer cadet company calling it the 1st West Drayton Guides. The 2nd West Drayton Company of Guides was formed in June 1916 and when the school left the district it was registered in April 1918 as the 1st West Drayton company. They helped twice a week in the factory canteen at the Hayes Munitions Factory carrying out a variety of tasks for which they were awarded the War Service Badge. At Hayes a Guide troop began in early 1917 and a scout group was also formed at the Jewish School in May 1918 when Mr. Percy Armytage, MVO, the Middlesex County commissioner, swore in members of the troop.

AIR-RAIDS

A new and frightening experience was about to take place. Never before had this country experienced air raids, but the United Kingdom was attacked by Zeppelins and bombers and, near the coast, by naval bombardment. Raids by plane were more destructive than the raids by Zeppelins, the main targets of which were defined as magazines, munitions factories, ports and garrisons.

No raids occurred nearby, but local inhabitants although seeing nothing of the actual bombing, could see Anti-Aircraft fire and Star Shells bursting over the capital and the neighbourhood, and heard a good deal including air-raid warnings given by the Signal Department of the Great Western Railway at Hayes. During night raids factories ceased production until the all clear was sounded and all trains, apart from those underground, were stopped.

The Commissioner of the Metropolitan Police issued letters to local Councils in May 1915 as to air-raid precautions. They advised that the public took refuge in houses so as to be out of the way of falling fragments of shells fired at enemy aircraft. All windows and doors on lower floors were to be closed, so as to prevent the admission of deleterious gas. The local Police were supplied with tripods and poles to prevent traffic from entering roads in which houses might be damaged. Another letter from the Commissioner arrived in late July 1917 informing the Council that on the approach of enemy aircraft on the way to London, sound rockets could be fired from Fire Brigade Stations in the County of London and at certain Police Stations in the Metropolitan Police District outside the County.

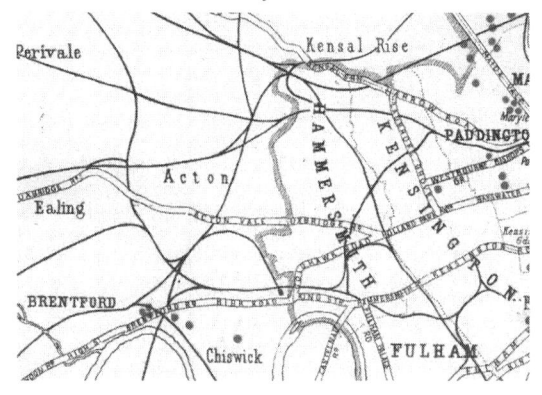

Where the bombs fell west of London (World War: 1914-1918 a Pictured History, edited by Sir John Hammerton)

An attempted raid by three German Zeppelins (two Army and the other Naval) on London and Hull on the night of 6th/7th June 1915 caused the heaviest casualties to date in Hull. None of the Army Zeppelins reached England, but near Ghent one of these Zeppelins was bombed in the air by Flight Sub-Lieutenant Reginald A. F. J. Warneford, whose maiden aunt lived at Uxbridge, after an hour-long chase. The craft burst into flames at about 2.30 am and fell onto a convent, killing all but one of her crew. The blaze was clearly seen by the VTC who were on duty that night. Explosions could also be heard from miles and miles away and even the sound of guns from the distant battlefields of France and Flanders could on occasions be heard when atmospheric conditions were right. When at 3.10 am on 7th June 1917, immediately before the British infantry assault, nineteen mines charged with over a million pounds on ammonal, which lay beneath the enemy position, erupted simultaneously from Ploegsteert to Hill 60, all along the Messines ridge, the noise of the explosion of a series of the largest and deepest mines ever used in warfare, could be heard. Again in July 1917 the guns from Belgium could also be faintly heard.

The first air-raid that seriously affected London took place on the night of Wednesday 8th September 1915 when two of three German Naval Zeppelins made landfall over the Norfolk coast. A few minutes later the explosion of bombs and the crackling of guns in the distance could be heard locally as bombs were dropped on Golders Green followed by more along a line from Euston to Liverpool Street. Many local people journeying in and around London saw the enemy craft and the bombs dropping. All of the twenty-six guns of the London defences and all searchlights were in action. In every raid, the hospitals were ready for any emergency, fire stations were prepared to respond to any call, every Special Constable had been called up, at every Police station surgeons and nurses had come on duty as had ambulance men with stretchers at the ready.

A Zeppelin raid took place in the night of 13th/14th October 1915. The L13, captained by Mathy the leader of the formation, swept round by St. Albans, but altered his course over Rickmansworth immediately after he had seen L.15 under fire, and headed south over the course of the river Colne, passing over Uxbridge and south of the modern London Borough on its way to Staines, and Guildford before making its way home, but not before dropping incendiary missiles at Woolwich. All of London's guns were in action. Despite the weather the slow, eerie, large cigar-shaped airship was audible as well as visible as it passed over the locality on its way to Chertsey. This raid was one of the deadliest of the war. In October 1915 churchwardens at Hayes received donations for insuring St. Mary's against damage by hostile aircraft.

The longest airship raid took place in East Anglia on the night of $2^{nd}/3^{rd}$ September 1916 when 16 Army and Navy Zeppelins airships attacked between the Humber and Ipswich. With the German army and navy combining for the first, and last, time to attack, this was the biggest airship raid of the war (it was also, for the Germans, an utter failure). It was to be the only time during the war that Army airships bombed the same target simultaneously. One airship, the SL II, commanded by Hauptmann Wilhelm Schramm, reached London, the place of his birth. Lieutenant William Leefe Robinson won his Victoria Cross on 2nd September 1916 for shooting down the SL11 at Cuffley in Hertfordshire. The flash of the exploding SL II could be seen over a radius of some 40 to 50 miles and despite the time being 02.25am it was seen by hundreds of thousands of cheering people. It was very clearly seen by the local men on duty and as some of the local trains were so late many inhabitants were able to see the spectacle themselves. Others were woken from their slumber by the sound of Anti-Aircraft fire and fled into the streets half-dressed as they had done before in moonlight raids and also were to do in later attacks. The news that an air attack was impending had spread all over London. Every vantage spot was crowded with spectators as dozens of beams from the searchlights showed from every part of London and the outer sections. London had never seen such brilliant illumination and there were loud cheers from high streets throughout the metropolis. The next day was a Sunday and the news spread quickly. Soon all the lanes around Cuffley were choked with sightseers – local roads too were soon crammed with those who knew that Lieutenant Leefe Robinson was the cousin of Rev. F.D. Sturgess, vicar of Yiewsley, and all local inhabitants kept their eyes wide open in case he paid a visit.

Another raid occurred at about on 24th September 1917 when Navy Zeppelins targeted the Midlands and northeast. Star Shells bursting in the air and lighting up the enemy's position could plainly be seen and the noise was awesome. At the same time Special Constables at Hayes were late for a Council Meeting because of the raid. Take-cover notices were evident in all the local villages. After this raid, huge rents were asked for locally.

These large Gotha aeroplanes also set out to bomb London, night after night from 28th September to 2nd October. They became known as the 'harvest moon raids'. Londoners had never heard such a bombardment as the raid which took place on 28th September and in the brilliant moonlight the barrage from north-west London was clearly visible.

On the night of 29th/30th January 1918 a number of attacks were carried out by hostile aeroplanes between 10pm and 12.30am. About 15 enemy planes, coming in small detachments, crossed the coast and four Giant aircraft headed for London.

It was about 8 in the evening when the warning of maroons was fired followed an hour later by the first guns. Most people made promptly for shelter but many continued in the streets until the guns were heard. The barrage guns were more distinctly heard in the district during this raid than ever before, but barrage fire was only violent in those districts where enemy planes were attempting to break through. Two machines reached London where one was viciously attacked near Tottenham and then headed for home, but not before dropping some bombs near Wanstead. Another aeroplane was attacked on its inward path, turned at Hertford and headed for Brentford where it dropped some bombs on the Ealing/Brentford border, killing 8 people. A salvo of guns in the neighbourhood proved the end of the raid. Another raid took place the following night. Public indignation had by now reached seething point.

London was the primary target for the night raid that took place on 16th/17th February 1918 and the local area was more than usually within the sound of the guns. Five German Giant aircraft had been dispatched and the Mercedes-engined Giants attacked Dover. During this air-raid, it was reported that some of the residents at Harlington sat up until the guns had finished and the raiders driven off.

There were more raids including one on the 25th April when Hayes Fire Brigade was called out for 1½ hours. When on the night of 19th/20th May 1918 over 40 German heavy bombers took off to bomb London, the sound of guns was fairly distinct locally. However, the flashes and rumbles of the aerial display were more impressive. During this raid, Hayes Fire Brigade was on duty for 3½ hours.

Between 1914 and the end of 1916 there had been 43 airship and 28 aeroplane attacks all over England. In mid October 1915, Hayes UDC insured Council premises against air-raids. By the end of hostilities, almost every part of London, apart from the west and south-west had been attacked. Between December 24th 1914 and June 17th 1918 there had been 51 airship raids and 57 aeroplane raids all over the country. A total number of 8,578 bombs had been dropped and by the end of the War, the total number of British air raid casualties amounted to 1,414 dead, 3,416 injured and material damage amounting to almost £3, 000,000. London suffered more than half of the casualties – 670 killed and 1,962 injured.

Many underground stations had become a refuge for panicking people, – as many as 300,000 on occasions whether raids were imminent or not, and some of those in tunnels were accommodated with gramophones by the Special Police. During a raid in the autumn of 1917 two Hayes residents were robbed of their purses while taking shelter in a tube station. After the air-raids of mid 1917, hundreds of air-raid refugees from London arrived in the district.

To begin with there were no air-raid shelters and air-raid warnings were unheard of. The Lights (London) Order placed restrictions on the lighting of London and 10 miles around after dark from the beginning of the war but this did not cover this area, so local Councils made their own arrangements. By early 1915 a policy of subdued lighting was adopted at Hayes. In late June 1915 councils received letters from the Metropolitan Police pointing out the advisability of extinguishing all street lights in the event of an air-raid. Gradually houses, factories, railways and trams were all brought under regulations tending to increase darkness. By the winter of 1916 every house and shop had its windows carefully shaded with dark curtains and the street lamps had been reduced in number and obscured so as to give no more than a glimmer of light and the headlights of vehicles were reduced in power.

Many summonses for showing light were brought against local people and local businesses. In August 1916, Hayes Council resolved to draw attention to the Metropolitan Police to the fact that during the air-raids that had recently taken place, the Gramophone Company had not extinguished lights until after gun-fire was distinctly heard. After an air-raid on 31st October 1917 lights had not been extinguished at the Beck Engineering Company works at Hayes End, by now a controlled company. The Ministry of Munitions enquired why the lights had not been extinguished. The Beck company replied that they had not received a warning that an air-raid was about to take place. In January 1918 under the Order the hour for the obscuration of lights was fixed for 6pm instead of 5.30. The local Police had noticed that many homes in the area had not properly obscured their windows and in January 1918 they drew this to the attention of the residents of Harlington through the local paper. Mr. Donnelly of Harlington was fined £1 for failing to shade windows at the Fairey Aviation Factory, Hayes, on 3rd March. James Neilson, of Redmead Road, Harlington, was fined 10/-, Church services were confined to daylight hours, as were theatres, restaurants and cinemas. The kerbs of many London streets were whitewashed so they could be visible to vehicles and pedestrians. People were also prosecuted for failing to have red lights on their cars.

There was a spate of road accidents caused by badly lit roads. After Summer Time was brought in, gradually things became more organised. Once the raiders were spotted there was usually about an hour's warning when an attack was imminent. In that time all the preparations had to be made. The searchlights and guns in London were manned nightly and always held ready, but when a raid was expected ambulances had to be mobilised, the Fire Brigade, which was still manned largely by volunteers, had to have all its strength available, including the engineer troops attached to it for rescue and demolition work, all the airmen to Stand To, the 'Specials' to be summoned and the hospitals warned. When air-raid warning bombs were heard local police patrolled the streets with whistles and 'Take Cover' notices. Maroons were fired, factory hooters blared out, church bells were rung and placards saying 'Warning!' were attached to bikes, motor bikes and cars. All of these were unavoidably associated with some alarm. Bugles were one way of sounding the 'All Clear'.

Local clocks, in common with other timepieces throughout the country including Big Ben, had all been stopped in the early days of the air-raids. Most of these were not to come on again until mid 1919.

REFUGEES and EVACUEES

During September 1914, a constant stream of Belgian refugees poured into England. By direction of the authorities, the refugees were quarantined and vaccinated. At first they arrived at Folkestone but in October, when it was seen that the German army would soon reach the coast, many thousands arrived at Dover. On their arrival in

London they were taken to a temporary haven in Aldwych. In the seven days beginning with 10th October, some 13,000 arrived, including 5,000 wounded Belgian soldiers. Within days of the outbreak of war preparations were being made to receive Belgian refugees, who in most cases were panic-stricken and had lost everything. Everywhere, doors were flung wide open to receive the destitute refugees. Thousands of offers poured in from people willing to house and feed them. Local houses were rented for the refugee families from the early days of the war and furnished by contributions. Residents of Uxbridge, Denham and elsewhere loaned a great deal of furniture. Councils excused properties occupied by the refugees, who worked for their livelihood and supported themselves, from paying rates.

The difficulties of classifying and registering the thousands of offers, the fitting of the guests to the hosts in batches of twos and threes, the temporary housing, the final dispatch of the refugees to country districts, all involved an immense labour. Local committees were formed, and there were soon 2,000 of them. Refugees were picked up from Aldwych where the Belgium Consulate had, early in the war, opened an office in General Buildings. Volunteer motorists conveyed many to their new homes. These volunteers became the Optimistic National Corps, Transport Section, then the Motor Squadron of the London Volunteer Rifles and eventually the National Motor Volunteers.

Many Lantern Lectures, Charity Concerts and other functions were held for the Belgian Relief Funds to which many of the refugees came. At Christmas 1914, Mrs. Roberts of The Firs, who also appealed for bicycles for the refugees, arranged a fancy dress dance at Herne House for the Belgians at Hayes, Dawley and Uxbridge. For local residents these were times to join in and to forget, albeit briefly, their troubles and enjoy themselves. Schools also held fund-raising events and made clothes for the refugee children.

The Parish Room at Hayes was set aside for refugees. Hearne House and lodge at Hayes, from the end of October 1914 was also used to accommodate refugees from Belgium. Also at Hayes, The Gables at Wood End was used for a short time as was Barra Hall. Cllr. Juan Collonna Drenon also took in a number of refugees at his home at Barra Hall Villa, Wood End. White Hall at Hayes End was also used. At Clayton Road school the children were asked to help find lodgings for the refugees. When it was suggested that different people (Belgians who had come to work at the Army Motor Lorries and Waggon Co. Ltd.) occupied the same bed day and night, not an unusual situation at that time, Mr. Heyward of the Dower House offered the use of a cottage in Harlington High Street as from the end of May 1915. Not all of the refugees stayed in the area. Some moved on – at least 6 moving to Southall by the spring of 1915.

About 100,000 Belgians fled to England after Germany invaded their country. These refugees did not establish new homes for themselves after the War but went back to Belgium.

HOUSING

The war put an end to residential building and the growth of outer London ceased. Hayes Council's plans to develop land for housing did not come to fruition. The Botwell Housing Scheme was put on hold and in 1919 was entirely scrapped.

Sunnyside Cottages, Harlington, c 1910
(Hillingdon Local Studies, Archives and Museum Service)

Large premises, including private houses, were taken over for various military purposes. Westcombe Lodge at Hayes, was taken over as a hospital. Barra Hall was used to station the Army cavalry while Lieutenant Colonel Alfred Reid of Barra Hall was serving with his regiment, the Yorks and Lancaster. The Royal Defence Corps, the 115th Protection Company, were stationed at Hayes and had been there since at least June 1916.

Rooms in houses were used to billet soldiers, although there was a regulation that soldiers would not be billeted in the house of the wife of a soldier serving abroad. For instance, in mid August 1914 soldiers were billeted at and around Uxbridge as part of the general scheme for the outer defence of London. Almost 20,000 men were placed between

Harrow, Uxbridge and Slough. The billeting of soldiers became law and many prosecutions took place.

Landlords within a 10 mile radius of London were given an allowance to help with rent, but this did not apply to any part of this Borough but it did apply to most parts of Ealing, and bad feeling was rife. There were heated debates concerning what some thought was a loss of their 3s 6d. Rents rose significantly in 1915, but were soon controlled by law and put back to pre-war costs so that extortionate rents could not be asked.

The influx of Belgian refugees and serving men as well as houses taken over as hospitals, all aggravated the serious housing shortage everywhere and after the first of the Zeppelin raids on this country when air-raid refugees fled the capital, the demand for accommodation outside the capital became urgent. Following the autumn 1917 raids people came out of London, mainly from the East End, to the Uxbridge and Hayes areas by tram in very large numbers, many of them bringing mattresses and pillows. As further demand for apartments rose drastically in this district fabulous prices were being offered. However, a large number of people, especially women with children, coming to the district from London to escape air-raids could not find sleeping accommodation and walked the streets at night.

Everywhere was crowded out and similar conditions were experienced all up and down the lines of the GWR and the Metropolitan railways.

Munitions workers who flooded in from almost anywhere, especially after 1915, when the National Filling Factories were built, preferred to lodge with families. Housing was at a premium. A scheme to bring 600 Scottish girls to work in the filling factories at Hayes without a thought of where they were going to be housed let alone what they were going to do in their spare time or what they were going to eat, and the extension of The Gramophone Company's premises, supplying additional jobs aggravated the situation. Although good wages compensated for the travelling time, due to the desperate housing situation everywhere, rents were increased and evictions rife. It was estimated that the number of people working in the Hayes district was 20,000 per day and 15,000 per night as and a consequence the sewerage and filtration facilities had been absolutely overpowered. In a field close to the Filling Factory, a huge number of cylinders of acid which belonged to the Admiralty were stored. RNAS ratings were posted there in charge of the cylinders. They were also in need of accommodation. The building of the United Glass Company at Botwell had made matters worse. In the spring of 1917, a Local Government Board's enquiry disclosed that although the Botwell area had become 'wonderfully developed', war officials and managers had been high-handed in dealing with the local inhabitants.

In Yeading the scheme to construct working class dwellings and to replace White's Row were halted and by 1915 the house dearth in the Hayes area had become much worse.

In 1915 the Medical Officer of Health for the Urban District of Hayes recorded that housing accommodation for the *'industrial classes in the District is undoubtedly insufficient'* He went on to say that there were many occupied cottages quite unfit for human habitation and closing orders had been issued for a number of them.

However, owing to the scarcity of dwellings, the Council did not proceed to demolition. During 1915, 21 houses suitable for habitation by the 'industrial classes' had been erected during the year by private enterprise. The housing situation was so chronic that in mid 1916, Hayes Urban District Council contacted the Local Government Board for a contribution towards the cost of the Botwell Housing Scheme and was preparing to present to them a scheme for Hayes, after having had a meeting at the Council Offices with the local employers. Most, if not all of the local local councils had also contacted the Local Government Board with the same request of a loan to build houses from about 1916 onwards to alleviate the housing situation in their areas. In their usual fashion the Board replied that they were unable to sanction any loan for a housing scheme.

In December 1917 the MOH reported that he much regretted *'that owing to the present conditions occasioned by the War, the Council has been unable to proceed with the erection of cottages at Yeading and near Botwell as proposed and sanctioned. The wretched unsanitary conditions of the cottages in White's Row, Yeading, is a disgrace to the district and a fertile soil for the development of consumption and rheumatism. The number of houses suitable for habitation by the industrial classes erected by private enterprise is......Nil'* By 1918 the Council had still been unable to increase accommodation as they had not managed to obtain the consent of the Authorities to raise the necessary loans, and the number of houses erected by private enterprise was only 15.

Only 50,000 houses were built in Great Britain, during the war, including those built for war workers. 10,000 permanent houses were constructed in connection with 38 munitions factories – some houses were not always built in areas appropriate to peacetime needs. In the spring of 1915, 1,200 dwellings were being erected in a new 'munition-workers' town' at Well Hall Station, near Woolwich. Early in 1916 the Local Government Board and the Ministry of Munitions were erecting private dwellings near Holmbury at Botwell without the permission of Hayes UDC., and the War Agricultural Committee had set up bungalows near Redleaf, which had to be demolished within 6 months after the Declaration of Peace as they had not been constructed in accordance with the Byelaws. That same year, two bungalows with wooden frames on brick foundations were also built on Mr. Shackle's land on the east side of Station Road. Two officials from the filling factory, who also designed and supervised the construction, occupied them. By early 1917 there was a Church Army rest hut at Botwell with sleeping accommodation. Shortly afterwards, temporary additions to the rest hut were approved by the Council. Female labour was arriving at Hayes at the rate of between 400 and 500 a week by February 1917. In order to alleviate the situation, a hostel at King's Hall at Southall was opened at the beginning of October 1917 for the use of the female members of staff at Hayes Filling Factory, although Southall also had a huge shortage of accommodation. In August 1918 the need of providing accommodation for the women forced the authorities to take over the rear of King's Hall for sleeping purposes. By September 1918 the Filling Factory was still taking on a very large number of women. Local papers in the area were asked to place adverts for accommodation in their pages. Most of the girls from the North and the Midlands were found lodgings in the Southall and Ealing districts.

With the influx of so many people, the Government encouraged local authorities to provide more housing, although up to this time it was the popular belief that private builders would continue to provide all normal housing needs. This, however, had proved impossible and with the lack of house building, serious problems were encountered after the war.

Clayton Road, Hayes (Hillingdon Local Studies, Archives and Museum Service)

SCHOOLS

The 1902 Education Act provided for the establishment of education other than elementary. Up until this time the only secondary schools had been private. The War put a stop to the flow of educational progress and after the war the country's financial difficulties permitted few improvements.

It was the infants' schools and junior schools which seemed to suffer the most because of the air-raids. On several occasions during raids affecting

London the attendance of the children fell. In the spring of 1915 a circular was issued by the Middlesex Education Committee advising schools in the county to immediately prepare a plan of action in the case of air-raids. It was advised that in the event of a raid the children should carry on working but be as far away as possible from the windows. They would not be released from the school until it had been ascertained that all danger had passed. The Committee also advised a strongly worded letter be sent to all parents informing them that they would be unable to collect their children at such a time. Each school differed in its drilling arrangements. In some when a whistle was blown the children had to lie flat on their stomachs; in others children were told to get under a desk. The Police were asked to give as long a notice as possible to schools in the event of an impending air-raid. New air-raid instructions, dated 23rd July 1917, were sent to all schools, which cancelled air-raid drills in force and advised them of the drilling of school children in preparation of air-raids. Children living in roads close to the school were to be sent home and children who were living in roads too far from the school were to remain in the school and remain sheltered - in the basement if there was one, unless written instructions to the contrary were received from their parents or guardians.

In the spring of 1915, the Chairman of the Education Committee authorised pupils over the age of 13 to be excused (not legally exempt from school attendance) from attending at school for the purpose of agricultural or Government work on the following conditions:-

1. The child was over the age of 13

2. The wages were satisfactory
3. Any child excused must return to school of they give up this work before he or she reaches the age of 14

Local authorities were under intense pressure to suspend the school attendance by-laws so that children could be released to undertake 'national work' and there was also a marked increase in early school-leaving to go to work. Summer holidays were mostly changed from August to July so that schoolchildren could help with the harvest. In the spring of 1918 the Education Committee informed all schools that it was not advisable to grant further exemption for work on the land to children between 13 and 14 'because of the evil results which follow'.

Church Walk, Hayes (Hillingdon Local Studies. Archives and Museum Service)

Most school children saved money that was collected for war savings and also contributed most willingly to fund raising and making 'comforts' for the troops – although not everything was appreciated by the Tommies.

Schooling suffered many interruptions. From almost the start of the war, Belgian refugee children attended local schools and the adults were given lessons in English. Air-raid refugees were also housed locally and it is known that their children were admitted to Emmanuel School, Northwood and Ickenham National School in October 1917 and another 10 in late February 1918. Local authorities were under intense pressure to suspend the school attendance by-laws so that children could be released to undertake 'national work' and there was also a marked increase in early school-leaving to go to work. Summer holidays were mostly changed from August to July so that schoolchildren could help with the harvest.

By 1916, the price of paper had almost trebled. To save paper, school magazines reduced in size or were not printed at all and slates had to be used wherever possible.

The 1902 Education Act provided for the establishment of education other than elementary. Up until this time the only secondary schools had been private. The War put a stop to the flow of educational progress and after the war the country's financial difficulties permitted few improvements.

Most school children saved money that was collected for war savings and also contributed most willingly to fund raising and making 'comforts' for the troops – although not everything was appreciated by the Tommies.

For schools the difficulty of the war years was mainly a matter of staffing. Great difficulty was experienced by school managers in filling temporary vacancies, owing to men enlisting in the services. Managers were not allowed to fill such vacancies permanently and it was exceedingly difficult to get any really competent teacher to accept a temporary post. Towards the end of 1915 the headmasters of schools with an average attendance of no more than 350 were encouraged to take a class. In early 1916 it was reported that out of a total of well over 200 teachers in Middlesex County elementary schools, only 10 had not joined the Colours or attested under the Derby scheme and in the secondary schools, out of 229 teachers, over 200 had enlisted or attested. By May 1918 more than 22,000 teachers had left the schools for the Colours, after a further call was made on the teaching profession made by the Board of Education and the National Service Ministry. A few men under 25 and a rather larger number under 32 had been kept in the schools by local education authorities as being indispensable. These were now to be called up and a serious situation was expected in the schools. The Middlesex Education Committee requested that in the *'present crisis the staffing of the Schools should be on the basis of the actual Code requirements wherever possible and the Committee would be glad if the Managers could see their way to release one of their teachers to assist in other schools if necessary'*.

Head teachers often gave news of teachers and pupils and were very sad when they had to report the deaths on active service of former pupils or staff. Mr. F. Hankins, an assistant master at Harlington School, was dismissed from the army suffering from severe shell-shock in 1916. He died in late 1918 at his brother's home in Montreal. He had served as a sergeant. Raymond Rodda was educated at the same school. After leaving he had become a coppersmith at the Gramophone Works. He had joined the Royal

West Kent Regiment on 1st September 1916 and served with the Expeditionary Force in France from 1st June 1917. He died of wounds received the previous day, on 17th September 1917 at No. 19 Casualty Clearing Station in northern France. Robert Howard, who lived at The Poplars situated in the High Street at Harlington, was a war dispatch rider during the evening but during the day he put in a hard day's work at the National Schools. He died at Hounslow Cottage Hospital in August 1918 after falling ill.

The little school at Cranford lost at least two former pupils, Edward Appleton who died of disease in Mesopotamia and Ted Bates, who had lived with his grandmother, Caroline Spring in the village.

At Hayes Council School, Mr. Ellis' eldest son was on active service. Mr. B.J. Miller, who had begun teaching there in July 1914, left the school to join up on 21st April 1915 and notification arrived at the school on 31st July 1916 that he had been killed in action in France. He had been in the fighting in the Dardanelles and had spent some time in Egypt. Later, news was received that he was wounded and taken prisoner by the Germans. Another teacher, Frank Butler, was a Corporal in the Royal Army Medical Corps. Mr. Pickering, a master at Dr. Triplett's School, whose wife was also a schoolmistress there at some time, lost two sons – Alfred and Robert, known by his middle name, Cecil. Both had been gone on to be educated at Uxbridge County School (as had Cecil's twin sister, Dorothy) and both were killed in action by a shell. Alfred was serving with the London Scottish and was killed on 28th March 1917, Cecil served with the Machine Gun Corps and was killed on 18th September 1918. Their cousin, Robert Pickering of Harmondsworth, was killed in action at Cambrai at the end of November 1917. A total of 41 former pupils from Dr. Triplett's School died on active service.

By July 1915, 46 boys of the Hayes Jewish School were in the fighting line and by the end of 1915 quite a number of 'old boys' had been wounded and four had been killed. George Cooper, the Drill Master at the School had worked at the school since 1912 and was shortly to be married to a Hayes girl. He had enlisted in the 16th Lancers as a corporal in 1914 and quickly rose to become a sergeant. He was killed in a pitiless rain of bullets on 12th October 1914. Mr. Smith, the then present instructor, a Reservist in the 7th Lancers who was with Mr. Cooper at the front, gave news of his death. The 'old boys' who had been killed up to that date were Moses Beckerwick who was killed at Ypres on 15th October 1914, aged 21; Myer Roseman who was killed in action at Neuve Chapelle on 12th March 1915; Private G. Garrett, RFA., who after being wounded returned to the trenches and was killed and Private D. Chapin of the 90th Winnipegs. Private Hyman, Canadian Infantry, had been severely wounded at Vimy in 1917. While he was in hospital he received the news that he was to be one of the recipients of four watches given by the School to those who had done well after leaving. By the end of hostilities, fourteen had been killed or died of wounds, forty-five had been wounded, two gassed and five prisoners of war. Eight gained the Military Medal (one with bar), one the DCM and one the Croix de Guerre. Two had also gained commissions. Clayton Road School at Hayes had three masters all on active service. Mr. Clark, senior master taught the top class. Lieutenant F.C.

Butler who taught history and geography amongst other subjects had served with the Duke of Wellington's Regiment in India. They all returned to the school a few months after demobilisation as did staff from other schools. Mr. Miller brought back lots of photographs.

They all returned to the school a few months after demobilisation as did staff from other schools.

The Gramophone Offices at Hayes 1912-1913, showing the machine shop being constructed. (Hillingdon Local Studies, Archives and Museum Service)

HEALTH

The early part of the 20th century saw the great reduction in the more serious infectious diseases and the civilian population did not suffer unduly during the war years. Surprisingly enough, the civilian death rate in Britain actually fell, although 1915 and 1918 were years of high mortality.

Cases of typhoid fever remained relatively constant in the industrialized world, and with the advent of proper sanitary facilities and with vaccines, was been virtually eliminated in many areas. In 1908 the total number of enteric fever cases in London was only 1,357 and all through hostilities there were sporadic cases of enteric fever throughout the locality.

Westcombe Lodge.
© Hayes and Harlington Local History Society

In anticipation of war, the Army Medical Services had 200,000 doses of the typhoid vaccine stored for army use. By the time of the end of the war, they had produced over 20 million doses.

A serum had been developed for the treatment of cerebro meningitis which was relatively rare in this country until 1915, although two deaths from the illness were reported at Hayes in 1914, when an epidemic spread and there were several reports of local cases, mainly affecting only individuals. A young child at Hayes died. In the County of London, 712 cases were notified and throughout England and Wales there were 2,343 cases. These were notifications amongst civilians only. In 1917, 3 cases of meningitis had been reported. A new and improved treatment arrived in 1918.

Scarlet fever had been a disease of great severity with a high death rate. Early in the 20th century however, it changed its virulence, causing, in the greater number of cases, a milder illness. A considerable outbreak of scarlatina in November 1914 mainly affecting those up to the age of 15, seriously strained the resources of the local isolation hospitals and convalescents were moved to cottage hospitals. Fifty-nine cases were reported at Hayes where the source of the original infection could not be traced but it was thought that it had spread by infection acquired at school. It affected only children up to the age of 15 and all but one was hospitalized. However, by the end of that year the numbers of notifications had significantly reduced and in the spring of 1915 there were only scattered cases and by mid June 1915 it was in decline. In that year there were 8 cases in the Hayes area. However, the last two years of the war 7 cases of scarlet fever were reported in 1917 and 8 in 1918. All these cases were treated in the Isolation Hospital in Kingston Lane, Uxbridge.

Diphtheria had been fairly widespread throughout the British Isles and had the greatest fatality rate, although mortality had greatly reduced after the introduction of an anti-serum which was first produced in some quantity in 1894. It came into general use in 1895. In 1914 three cases of the disease were reported at Hayes where the source of the infection could not be traced. In 1915 diphtheria was prevalent throughout the country and was the largest case of all infectious diseases for that year. In that year there were a total of 30 cases reported in the Urban District of Hayes. Twenty eight sufferers were taken to the Isolation Hospital where 9 died. The Medical Officer at Hayes was empowered to incur any necessary expenditure in taking swabs and disinfecting schools. In a two week period in November 1915 there was an outbreak in which 17 cases were reported at Harlington. They were taken to the Isolation Hospital where the total number from Harlington numbered 22. Daily bulletins on the conditions of the patients were posted up in Harlington to save enquiries. By December 1915 there was a serious outbreak of diphtheria in the district. Another outbreak of diphtheria in 1916 and the increase in Harlington's population made the need for proper sanitation urgent but this had been put on hold. Dawley Infants' School closed because of the outbreak at Harlington from 17th May until 31st May 1916. One case of diphtheria was reported at Hayes in the spring of 1917. Another outbreak of diphtheria at Harlington was noted in August 1917 and the total number of cases at Hayes for that year was 5 and in 1918, 7.

In 1872 there had been a severe epidemic of the dreaded smallpox. In the following year, a huge number of people were vaccinated, but despite the effectiveness of the vaccine outbreaks of the disease still frequently occurred. A large outbreak began in Great Britain in 1901. In early November 1901, notifications rose to 227 and by January 1902 this had grown to reach 546 in a fortnight, of cases occurring all over London. By 1906 this outbreak had died down. From then on the severe smallpox in any period was very small and never became a serious Public Health problem again. During this war, about 7,000,000 people, mainly adult males, were vaccinated during their time in the Forces. This prevented the importation of the disease into the country and was welcomed by those believed that the disease could be effectively controlled by the vaccination of contacts. However, several local cases had been reported but in the spring of 1918 smallpox broke out in the district. Patients suffering from smallpox and other infectious diseases were taken to Yeading Smallpox Hospital and Kingston Lane

Hospital in Uxbridge. The Yeading Isolation hospital had an agreement with the Joint Hospital Board of other districts in Middlesex to reserve for their use a limited number of beds at the hospital in the event of an outbreak of smallpox. In April 1918 one patient from Hanwell was admitted. Many of the women employees in the National Filling Factory wore a red ribbon band on their left arm to show that they had been vaccinated against it.

Measles, a disease of high infectivity, continued unabated. There was an outbreak in the summer of 1914 and towards the end of the year. The last epidemic had been in the last quarter of 1912 and the first quarter of 1913 and in 1913 the County of Middlesex had recorded a total of 377 deaths from measles – the highest recorded since 1900. In the spring of 1915 measles was prevalent, although in that year only one death was recorded at Hayes – that of a toddler - and it contributed to the upward serge in infant mortality and rose again from 1916-1917. In 1917, 34 cases were reported and in 1918 was there an epidemic.

Tuberculosis had declined during the latter part of the 19th century, but was still prevalent. It rose during the war partly due to poor housing and overcrowding, exhausting work and worry over the dreaded knock on the door. The disease easily spread with the influx of many people, but hospital beds were given to soldiers rather than tubercular civilians. In 1915, 5 cases were reported in the Hayes Urban District with one death, in 1917, 12 and in 1918, 9 cases were reported. Spitting mugs were provided free by the Hayes Council.

In early 1918 the Medical Officer at Hayes noticed a large number of cases of gastric ulcer and other districts had also noticed the growth. It was not thought that the diet at that time had anything to do with this increase, although many people in October 1917 were complaining about the ill effects of war bread. Overall bread consumption dropped by 22% under rationing.

Mental health suffered with the strain that any war brings. The noise, sleepless nights and anxiety of the air-raids and bombings- although these amounted in the end to almost nothing more than a nuisance- the war diet, the fear that came with every knock at the door, or for those better off, the long-distance telephone call, and the dread of the bad news that could arrive at any moment if it hadn't already done so, left lots of people drained.

In December 1917 the Medical Officer of Health for the Urban District of Hayes reported that the in his opinion the unsanitary conditions of the cottages in Yeading were a disgrace to the district and a fertile soil and damp subsoil led to the development of consumption and rheumatism. Many areas, even at this time, had bad sanitary arrangements, although in most places locally plans were already being acted upon. The Local Government Board had been founded in 1871 and had done much useful work in the sphere of sanitation up to the end of the 19th century. Its president at that time was Dr. Christopher Addison. However, it was by the end of the War outdated and agitation sprang up for the creation of a Minister of Health. Dr. Addison introduced a Bill which became law on 3rd June 1919.

It is thought that American soldiers unwittingly took the 'Spanish flu' with them into the war, although others suspect it began in 1916 in one of the many hospitals around Etaples on the Somme.

By June 1918 it had arrived in Great Britain, peaking in the second week of July and again in the first week of November. The final wave of this new strain of 'Spanish flu' appeared towards the end of January 1919, peaking in the last week of February that same year. It was secondary pneumonia that killed rather than the flu itself. It was one of the worst plagues in history. People wore masks in streets and in some towns, roads were sprinkled with disinfectants. Queues formed outside chemists' shops for medicines. In London leaflets advising preventative measures were distributed to every house. Estimates differ but there were probably over 22,000,000 deaths worldwide, 250,000 in Britain. By October 1918 ranks of the police had been thinned. Public institutions were thoroughly disinfected. The illness affected everybody alike. William Leefe Robinson, VC., had been taken prisoner in April 1917 when his plane was shot down near Lens in France by a German flight led by the 'Red Baron'. He arrived back in England on 14th December 1918 and died on 31st December 1918 at Stanmore. He is buried at Harrow Weald. Closer to home, previously healthy 14 year old Joseph Spooner who lived at 1 Sheraton Hostel in Hayes died of the disease as did Henry Laws of Pinkwell Farm, a Private with the 13th Royal Fusiliers. He died of influenza followed by pneumonia at Hounslow Military Hospital on 22nd November 1918, aged 22. He had joined the Army in November 1915 and went to France early in 1916 with the 20th Manchesters and later transferred to the Labour Corps. He is buried at Harlington.

Local Pensions Committees were set up in 1916 to deal with the training and treatment of disabled men, report on appeals against the findings of the Ministry of Pensions that incapacity was not due to service, deal with applications for alternative pensions by men and widows, make special allowances to wives and dependants in need and grants to meet sickness in a soldier's family etc. Servicemen posted as missing in action were not declared officially killed until up to one year had passed and a military tribunal heard the facts relating to the disappearance. If the loss of records meant that a date could not officially be declared, then an arbitrary date was decided upon. A notification of 'missing in action' meant an immediate loss of income and the uncertainty of any pension rights, which was so devastating to the family of a married man.

Many hospitals became inundated with injured soldiers and could hardly cope with civilian casualties.

Concerns had been voiced for improvements to public health. One of the priorities was the fight against infant mortality. By 1918 there was a downward trend. Gradually medical arrangements were developed. In 1918 dental and medical clinics for schoolchildren were planned up and down the country but most seem to have been unacceptably delayed. Early in 1918 a Health Visitor was appointed for Hayes and Yiewsley conjointly. The Health Visitor was to spend 3 days at Hayes and 2 days at Yiewsley. One month later a Maternity and Child Joint Welfare Committee was appointed at Hayes, as suggested by the Local Government Board. By the end of 1918 the Government were committed to the idea of a new Ministry for Health to co-ordinate the service for health and national insurance and to take over the duties of the Local Government Board.

HOSPITALS

The flow of casualties from the various theatres of war soon overwhelmed the existing medical facilities in the United Kingdom. The War Office had military hospitals erected in favourable districts, towns set aside parts of their infirmaries for the wounded and in some cases built hospitals and handed them over fully equipped to the military authorities. Many wealthy people converted their residences into hospitals and bore sole charge and others handed their houses over to the Red Cross Society, or to be used as hospitals or places of convalescence.

On the outbreak of War, Southampton became the No. I Military Embarkation Port, and the port of departure for the British Expeditionary Force, as all railway lines led directly or indirectly to it. The first convoy of 111 sick and wounded men arrived here on 24th August 1914 and were taken in the War Department Ambulance Train to the Royal Victoria Hospital, Netley. The new Marine station at Dover, which had not yet been completed, was ready on 2nd January 1915 to receive up to two hospital ships and six ambulance trains at the same time. It had been a rush job to finish the Marine station. The stream of wounded from Flanders seemed never-ending and finally it was decided to complete the station within a week. Work started on 23rd December and by working day and night right through Christmas, the work was finished to schedule.

There were 4 ambulance trains in service in 1914. By July 1916 there were 28. Over 75 hospital ships were in service during the war. In the end the total number of sick and wounded British and Commonwealth servicemen from all theatres of war conveyed in ambulance trains from British ports up to April 1919 was 2,680,000, divided fairly equally between Southampton and Dover, apart from a small number landed at other ports. The vast majority of those arriving at Southampton and Dover were the wounded from France. Those from various Eastern campaigns were landed at Avonmouth, Devonport or Liverpool.

Ambulance men lined up at a station waiting to disembark the wounded. (H.W.Wilson, The Great War)

There were almost 200 railway stations in Britain which received convoys of the sick and wounded. Denham and Southall, on the Great Western Railway, were the nearest stations to this area which received military ambulance trains which had been sent from either Dover, the principal port for the transport of the wounded, or from Southampton, or from both.

The distribution of patients after their arrival in this country was complicated. Their destination depended very largely on the nature of their disability. It was essential that certain cases should go to

141

hospitals specialising in particular types of treatment. For instance, the chief place for face wounds was the Cambridge Hospital, Aldershot until 1917 when a new hospital for face injuries opened at Frognal near Sidcup in Kent. To begin with casualties returning to Britain would receive initial treatment in British hospitals, and would be transferred to convalescent hospitals to make way for new arrivals from the front. In many cases these were in large houses lent by their owners. Australian, New Zealand and Canadian casualties usually went to hospitals which their own medical personnel had established in Britain. South Africans were nursed at a military hospital at Richmond. Similarly Jewish servicemen were usually sent to the Beech House Military Hospital Brondesbury, London or the Mote Auxiliary Hospital, Maidstone, the two main hospitals that looked after that particular faith until the Tudor House Military Hospital at Hampstead Heath (which was the only hospital intended exclusively for the use of Jewish soldiers) opened in October 1918. It received a large number of patients until the middle of 1919.

To facilitate distribution, advanced information was cabled about the various categories of patients (lying and sitting patients) on each hospital ship and the estimated time of arrival. These categories were subdivided into the numbers of officers, nurses and other ranks, with further subdivisions into surgical, medical, infectious, mental, and any other special cases. Patients were labelled with one of the five areas corresponding to their home area – London and Southern, West of England, Midlands, North England and Scotland and Ireland. This meant there was a possibility that patients would be sent to a hospital close to where they lived. The area home commands showing the bed situation in their larger and specialist hospitals sent daily notification.

Private individuals generously offered their houses for the use of the wounded. The Admiralty and War Office had decided that most offers of houses for auxiliary hospitals should reach them only through the British Red Cross Society. A flood of offers (5,000) poured in. The Red Cross Society had an onerous task examining and sifting through all them. Several large houses and other institutions in the area were offered, including Mr. Robert Newman, auctioneer of Harlington, who offered Bourne House to the invalided soldiers.

It was for voluntary hospitals that VAD nurses had been recruited and trained, and it was in these hospitals - about 1600 of them countrywide - that most VADs spent their war service. These hospitals were set up to receive the sick and occasionally the wounded from the battlefields. At the end of June 1916 hospitals were ordered to clear out all convalescents and prepare for a huge rush of wounded. Most VADs were unpaid and worked full or part-time and were under trained nurses recruited locally or through the Red Cross from Devonshire House in Piccadilly, although it had been announced that the Red Cross nurses would not work in Middlesex. However, in September 1916 the War Office consented to accept uncertified women for work in military hospitals. They were called 'Special Service Probationers'.

The County Director of the Middlesex Territorial Force Association received all offers for the registration of temporary hospitals and detachments. In Middlesex by April 1916 there were

20 men's and 38 women's VADs with a total strength of almost 3000 of which over 1400 had been mobilised – men for transport and women for nursing in the auxiliary hospitals in the county of which by that time there were 21 with almost 1500 beds. The local VAD was often called upon to help with the removal of wounded soldiers – even from the other side of London. By the end of the war, the local VAD had assisted in the transport of thousands of men.

Westcombe Lodge, Lady Hillingdon's home for babies, situated in its own extensive grounds in the High Road, Hayes End, was offered by Lady Hillingdon as an equipped hospital with the intention to use it as the main hospital for the King's Royal Rifle Corps stationed at Denham, although a few of the injured also came from battlefields of Flanders. It was the first VAD hospital to be mobilised in Middlesex. Westcombe Lodge became a Military Hospital, often known as the Hillingdon VAD hospital, under the War Office staffed by the 2nd Middlesex VAD, who were mobilised in mid October 1914. Mrs. Craig was in charge. Doctor Lock, of Uxbridge, and Dr. Muspratt, of West Drayton, were the doctors in charge at that time. It had 5 large well-equipped wards with 20-25 beds, which looked out onto gardens and one operating theatre. A tent was erected on the lawn where the men spent much of their time so that they would not feel the change when they went back to camp. It had one trained sister and 32 ladies of the VAD. The equipment was provided by the VAD Supplementary and sheets, blankets, pillows, etc were donated by local people. By May 1916 it had dealt with over 530 patients. In November 1916 the hospital was registered under the War Charities Act. The Uxbridge VAD volunteered for duty at this hospital and always attended when called upon.

Hayes Fire Brigade 1913-1914
(Hillingdon Local Studies, Archives and Museum Service)

In mid January 1918 Uxbridge Ambulance Brigade was asked to help at the hospital and a week later members of the 43 Middlesex VAD (Uxbridge) acted as orderlies there. Very occasionally deaths took place at this hospital, perhaps none so poignant as the suicide whilst of temporary unsound mind of Harry Meyer Silverstein. He was a 22 year old Canadian cadet who was born at Winnipeg but stationed at Denham Camp who was found in a washhouse on the evening of Saturday 9th February 1918 with his throat cut. He was admitted to the hospital at 10.50 that night and his throat stitched to help his breathing. A doctor from Hounslow operated on him the next morning but he died shortly afterwards at about 12.55. He is buried at Willesden Jewish Cemetery.

Hayes Cottage Hospital had closed temporarily for some weeks when it reopened on 1st October 1915 with a new matron. Although still on alert during air-raids, it closed again in early 1917 'for an indefinite period' as the great demand for women for war work had left the hospital without a matron and there was also a lack of adequate financial support. Various fund-raising events to help fill the coffers took place. One of them was at the end of March 1917 when the GWR vocalists entertained at the Hayes YMCA Hut. It seems to have reopened in early 1918 with a nurse from London carrying out the duties of the matron, as on 16th February 1918 the National Aero Engines Factory Philanthropic and Loan Club held a Grand Concert at the Park Theatre, Hanwell, in aid of aid of Hayes Cottage Hospital funds.

The small cottage hospital situated in Sipson Lane, Harlington, serving Harlington, Harmondsworth and Cranford closed for 2 months from February 1918 when the matron resigned. In the space of one year –June 1915 to June 1916 it had treated only 31 patients, was extended after hostilities. An operating theatre formed part of this extension to the property, which was built as a memorial to the fallen of Harlington.

PRISONERS OF WAR

Prisoners of War were numbered in the millions and there were many charges on both sides that the rules, drawn up at an international conference at The Hague in 1899 and 1907, were not being observed.

The exact number of local men taken prisoner is difficult to establish. Some of them died from disease, starvation or dysentery. Civilians working abroad were also liable to be captured.

Mr. L. G. Beaumont of Harlington was captured early in the war (probably in early 1915) and was interned at Ruhleben, a race-track near Berlin. In about mid 1916, news arrived that Private W.A. James of Angel Lane was a prisoner in Germany where he encountered Mr. Walter Ansell, also of Angel Lane. At some time in 1917 Private W. Leonard Clements of Cranford, who had enlisted early in the war, was reported as missing in action. In November 1917 a short memorial service in his memory was held at the 'school chapel'. Days later news arrived at Cranford that he was a POW in Germany. Private Charles Watts of Blythe Road had taken part in the fighting at Cambrai on 20th November and was captured along with others at there on 30th November 1917. His first and only Christmas in captivity was miserable, dinner being one slice of bread and some cabbage water. Private W. Stonestreet, of Hayes, was taken prisoner eight months before the end of hostilities. In the spring of 1918 during the German spring offensive many other local lads were captured. In fact it had been noted that the numbers of POWs taken by the enemy had greatly increased since 20th March 1918 when the Germans began their spring offensive, including Private H. Deamer of the 2nd Wiltshire Regiment who lived at Hayes at 9 North Hyde Road, who had been captured on 9th April 1918 near St. Sixte while trying to stop the Germans from breaking through in front of Ypres and drive for the Channel ports.

After the armistice, those captured gradually returned home. Private Charles Watts, who was serving with the 8th Royal Fusiliers was in one of the first parties of POWs to arrive back in England. He came over on the *'Archangel'* from Rotterdam, arriving at Hull on 17th November 1918. Lieutenant T. Fairall, 20th Middlesex Regiment, of Hayes had been a POW since 9th April 1918 when the Battalion Headquarters in the right sub-sector Bois Grenier sector was surrounded by the enemy and was in Cologne at the time of the signing. He was in one of the first party of officers to arrive in England, coming home via Holland. Private E. Carter, son of Mrs. Carter of Hunt's Lane, Harlington, had been held in a German POW camp (not one of the better ones, he said), returned home at the end of January 1919. Celebrations were held everywhere to welcome home returning servicemen.

Local Prisoners of War Funds were set up early in the War, affiliated to the British Red Cross Fund through its Central Prisoner of War Committee. It was agreed that properly selected food should be sent to each prisoner once a fortnight and parcel should weigh 10lb with 13 lb. of bread. Although food parcels were sent to the men, it is doubted whether all were received. Unless a special label was affixed to the parcel, no Post Office would accept it and no individual could hand over a parcel there. In 1917 it was agreed that private parcels of food and clothing weighing up to 11lb from family and friends was allowed. The only centre for distribution in the whole of Middlesex was at Northwood. The Northwood Fund, which was registered under the War Charities Act 1916, began in June 1915, secured the responsibility of supplying parcels to prisoners in the Middlesex Regiment. In the period beginning June 1915 and ending in December 1916 they had dispatched 12 large cases and 750 parcels of food to 37 different prisoners, averaging one parcel per fortnight per prisoner. During 1917,

864 parcels were sent. By June 1918 £1170 had been collected together with gifts in kind and 72 parcels had been dispatched to 12 POWs that year. In May 1918 there was an appeal signed by the Duke of Bedford urging the claims of the Lord Lieutenant's County Fund for Middlesex Regiment's Prisoners of War of which there were 1,400 by the beginning of 1918. £17,000 was needed to support them.

Captured German POWs were held at many places in Britain. Denham Lodge at the Denham end of Uxbridge High Street accommodated Prisoners of War who could occasionally be seen in Uxbridge as they made their way by motor lorries to the Lodge. For a time German officers were also held at Eastcote. Denham Lodge and Eastcote, which was attached to Denham Lodge, were Agricultural Depots under Feltham. Other camps at The Needles, a large house at Northolt, Langley Park at Iver Heath and Stoke Green at Stoke Green, Bucks, were also Agricultural Depots attached to Denham Lodge under Feltham. Not surprisingly, many of the men were hired out to local farmers, as they were at Harlington in the autumn of 1917 when the shortage of local labour necessitated them harvesting potatoes and at Harefield in the autumn of 1918. Prisoners also helped at Lowe and Shawyers Nursery and were working on the roads, like at Sipson in 1917 and (again) at Harlington in May 1918. Working Camps were also under Feltham, but there were none in this area. By the autumn of 1918 there were between 700 and 800 Germans employed in Middlesex.

ALIEN INTERNEES and SPY FEVER!

Britain interned between 29,000 and 30, 000 foreigners during the 1914-18 period, most of

149

them were German Jews. Many had settled in this country long ago or had sought political refuge here. Unfortunately it was a disaster with anti-civilian excesses. However, unlike some other districts, the locality appears to have remained almost unaffected.

A large number of aliens had been interned on account of 'spy fever'. Twenty 'known spies' were arrested before war was declared on 4th August, with a further 200 people rounded up four days later. It was later claimed that this had broken up a German spy ring. The Aliens Restriction Act had come into force on 5th August 1914, which required all aliens to register with the police. Numerous 'aliens' who had not registered were taken to court where the fines were usually heavy. On 5th September the Home Office and War Office decided that it was necessary to intern all male Germans aged between 17 and 55. By 13th September this was suspended, as there was no more space to hold them!

Eugene Sandow, was born Frederick Muller in Konigsberg, East Prussia, on 2nd April 1867. He was a celebrated strong man, and a naturalized Englishman. He commissioned a factory for the production of cocoa in Hayes which was built by John Mowlem and Co. and was up-to-date in every respect. Sandow's Cocoa and Chocolate Co. Ltd., was completed in 1914 and stood on just over 38 acres bounded by Great Western Railway and the Grand Junction Canal. Hayes Station was close at hand and the Great Western Railway had scheduled a strip of land alongside their line for the compulsory purchase of widening their line, and the Government commandeered a vacant portion of the site for military purposes for the period of the war. Railway siding had been put in and a road (Sandow Road) was built from the factory to Hayes Station. The building was of about 10,000 sq.ft. and consisted of 3- storeys. Orchards and market gardens surrounded it. Late in 1914 Mr. Sandow was interned, even though he had offered 500 silver-plated 'cocoa sets' free to the families of any serving men who drove the Germans out of France, and his factory confiscated and in October 1916 the factory was compulsorily liquidated. It was taken over by the Peter-Cailler-Kohler Concerne, a Swiss-owned company, and renamed the Hayes Cocoa Company.

By late August 1914 Robert Oberfahren, an unemployed German subject of Keith Road, Hayes was charged with being an alien German enemy in possession of a revolver and 23 cartridges without lawful excuse or permission, contrary to the Aliens Restriction Act 1914. The Uxbridge Police Court sentenced him to 3 months in prison. In early November 1914 another German was arrested at Botwell and taken to a concentration camp.

Anti-German feeling was whipped up by the Press and politicians and further fuelled by the sinking of three British cruisers, the *'Aboukir'*, *'Hogue'* and *'Cressy'*, on 22nd September 1914. In some cases Germans were interned for their own safety.

Although the problems of where to hold the aliens remained, by 20th October the internment of Germans, Austrians and Hungarians had started again. Accommodation was at a number of different camps – Beech Abbey, Hampshire; Douglas, Isle of Man and various old liners moored in the Thames estuary. The closest to home was at Olympia where conditions were rough and ready. By early November 1,500 men were held at Olympia while the total throughout Britain had reached 10,000. The continued rise in internees prompted the Home Office to join the War Office in a search for other camp sites. By the spring of 1915 there were some 19,000 aliens in internment, some of whom had been taken to large camps such as that established at Alexandra Palace. A great many were also taking up valuable space in local prisons throughout the country. At the end of February 1915 Knockaloe on the Isle of Man was available with accommodation for 2,000 men, which was increased to 5,000 men in November.

By 1915 19,000 German aliens had been interned. The sinking of the Lusitania in May 1915, in which one person from West Drayton was killed, further fuelled anti-German feeling and in less than one week the Prime Minister, Herbert Asquith announced that all alien men of fighting age were to be interned. Knockaloe would have to be extended. By the end of 1915 the 20,000 capacity of Knockaloe had been reached. By the end of 1915 there were almost 30,000 internees, internments having risen at a rate of 1,000 men per week. Although the largest camps remained on the Isle of Wight other smaller ones were scattered throughout England and Scotland, including Reading Jail, Stratford, Islington, Alexandra Palace, Frimley in Surrey and Olympia.

Anti German societies sprang up. The nearest seems to have been at Harrow where the Anti-German Association was vehemently welcomed.

Startling revelations surfaced in April 1916 when Israel Eremlard, of The Bungalow, Clayton Road, Hayes, a Russian subject, was remanded at Uxbridge Police Court with causing grievous bodily harm to Scharl Zander. On 13th April

Eremlard struck Zander on the head with an iron blow-pipe at the Sheraton Glass Works at Hayes. At the subsequent trial it was discovered that Zander, who was German, had come into the country in 1912 as a glass cutter. His internment had been arranged by the police but it had proved difficult to recruit anyone for his class of work. The Home Office advised Zander's internment.

1918 saw a renewed public outcry for the internment of all enemy aliens, whether naturalised or not.

Authorisation for the release of wartime detainees came in the New Year of 1919 and arrangements were made for their repatriation. A few remained in England until the end of 1919, their personal particulars recorded as required by the Aliens Act.

ARMISTICE! - Monday 11th NOVEMBER 1918

On Monday 11th November 1918, the day of the Armistice, it was dreary and wet. Hostilities in the west had ceased at 11am French time, but the last four years, fourteen weeks and two days had taught everyone to be patient. Many false hopes and rumours had circulated before. Eleven o'clock came and went. A surprising silence had descended when suddenly guns, hooters, horns etc blared. Just before midday, as news of the armistice spread workmen downed tools and most school children were given a half-day holiday. Joyful crowds full of hysterical jubilation were cheering, whistling and singing and commandeered vehicles of every description. Drapers were besieged with people buying Union Jacks, which they hung from bedroom windows. All kinds of musical instruments appeared as if by magic. Patriotic songs were the order of the day. Trams were so crowded that it was impossible for the fares to be collected. This good-natured rowdyism lasted until the Saturday night. Perhaps the most striking thing was the lighted streets and no worry about Special Constables coming to knock at the door. Huge bonfires were lit after dark, but it started raining heavily and the fires were put out.

In Uxbridge a notice confirming the Armistice was posted in the widow at the Gazette office just after 10.30 in the morning where a small crowd had gathered. A cyclist rode around shouting out the news.

At the National Filling Factory at Hayes, maroons and hooters blared. Tools were downed and a general holiday was either proclaimed or taken. The girls from the factory were adorned with red, white and blue ribbons. Thousands of workers made their way to the station where hawkers were selling flags and souvenirs. Station Bridge was one mass of cheering and singing people. Mouth organs, banjos and other musical instruments appeared and were played. A couple of soldiers near Hayes Station were surrounded by a crowd of girls and were not allowed to carry on their way until all had been kissed. Local children had no idea that War was over, although they knew something was afoot when they heard the Gramophone Works hooter which had unusually been going off many times. At Clayton Road School in Hayes at about 11.15am the headmistress, Miss Hyde, came into the classrooms to tell the children that the Germans had surrendered and that War was over. They were told to go home and need not return until the morning, unless they wanted to. Dawley Infants' School had closed on 4th

November 1918 because of an outbreak of influenza and reopened on 11th November with a fair attendance in the morning but practically empty in the afternoon. At Harlington, the church bells were out of order, so the ringers improvised with the remaining five bells until someone came to repair the sixth. Union Jacks, the Stars and Stripes, the French Tricolor and other flags adorned flagstaffs and rooftops.

The guns had fallen silent. The 'war to end all wars' was over and peace was here at long last but the cost had been high. Death on such a scale had never been witnessed before. Almost 1,000,000 Britons has lost their lived. Civilian losses, apart from those who perished in air-raids, amounted to 15,000 deaths among the crews and passengers of merchant and shipping vessels. Mrs. and Miss Everall of Blyth Road, Hayes, were lost in mid March 1917 when the boat they were travelling on back to England was torpedoed by a German submarine.

Everywhere things gradually began to turn back to normal, although some things that had been abandoned never returned and others took some time to return. For instance, the choirs of St. Margaret's, Uxbridge, and St. Andrew's, Uxbridge, St. John's Uxbridge Moor, Cowley, Yiewsley, West Drayton, Harmondsworth, Harlington Hayes, Ruislip and Harefield had met annually for a festival service at Hillingdon on St. John the Baptist day – June 24th. They had last met in 1913 and did not reconvene until 1923.

Of the seven million men who went to fight, a tenth of them never returned – almost a whole generation had been wiped out. The War Memorials show that Hayes lost 93 men, including several sets of brothers; 14 from the Hayes Jewish Industrial School which had had 1 officer and 139 men on active service, and over 40 'old' Dr. Triplett's boys perished. 32 men from Hayes Baptist Chapel took part in the war of whom four died. 22 members of Hayes CIB served in the war. 5 were killed, 11 wounded and 3 taken prisoner. The memorial at St. Dunstan's Church at Cranford records 20 names, three were brothers, Archibald, Frederick and Harry Lipscombe.

Their names will live forevermore.

THE WAR MEMORIALS

CRANFORD WAR MEMORIAL

ST. DUNSTAN'S CHURCH

The dedication of the Cranford War Memorial tablet and stained glass window took place at Easter in April 1920 in an evening service at St. Dunstan's Church. The tablet is simple in form, executed in marble of two colours. A window stands immediately above the tablet and represents the figure of St. George. The tablet cost £65 and the window £85. A permanent memorial to Reginald Roots, the late scoutmaster who died of gas wounds at Netley on 9th October 1916, was unveiled in January 1917 on a wall in the scout hall, on his 23rd birthday. The memorial comprised an enlarged life-like photograph of the late scoutmaster in the uniform of the London Scottish, his regiment, and an illuminated memorial tablet, the gift of Mr. Percy Armytage, MVO.

In January 1919 a well-attended public meeting was held where it was proposed to erect an institute in the village as a War Memorial Hall. Five months later, Mr. Henry Morland offered a piece of land opposite his own house, extending to the Avenue, with a frontage of 45ft. In mid 1920 a building in Southall was purchased, pulled down and reerected and a lean-to was constructed at the eastern end to afford additional accommodation. The hall was opened on Wednesday December 13th 1920.

HAYES WAR MEMORIALS

HAYES WAR MEMORIAL
Funds for a memorial were being raised by early 1919. The memorial was to be 'of a utilitarian character'. In the autumn of 1920 the residents of Hayes were given five schemes – a children's corner in the then new recreation ground; a shelter or clock; a reading room and library; a clock tower on the then new housing site; almshouses or a club and social welfare centre for ex-servicemen and relatives, of which they were to choose only one. Eventually a memorial in the Churchyard and a tablet in the Church were chosen. It was situated in Church Road, Hayes, and was in the form of a wooden cross on a stone plinth with inscriptions commemorating both World Wars on the surrounding walls.

There was also in Hayes Parish room a record of the 22 members of St. Mary's CIB who served in the war 1914-1918. 5 were killed, 11 wounded and 3 take prisoner.

HAYES SALEM CHAPEL
Thirty two men from the little Baptist Church at Hayes took part in the war, and of these four made the great sacrifice. On a morning in mid December 1919 an oak Communication table was placed in the church, bearing the names of two prominent members of the church, Eric Leonard Chambers and Stanley Harris Gregory. The table was unveiled by Alderman C.F. De Salis, Chairman of the Middlesex County Council. The church is no longer in existence.

ST. JEROME'S CHURCH

A colourful hand illustrated Roll of Honour in a carved oak frame commemorates men who attended the church who died on active service during the First World War. The frame was the gift of Lady Seabrooke in mid 1919, and her own handiwork. The writing and illuminating was designed and carried out by Mr. W. Ham, of Plymouth, free of all cost.

HAYES URBAN DISTRICT COUNCIL

Hayes UDC's memorial was in the form of two oak panels containing the names of those who fell during the war, affixed to either side of the entrance to the Council offices in Barra Hall. Mr. Liddall provided the oak boards for the panels which were affixed in place in late 1917 and the names of the deceased were added as and when.

THE GRAMOPHONE COMPANY

A brass plaque in memory 75 of the company's staff who died during World War One is kept in the company's premises at Hayes.

Dr. TRIPLETT'S SCHOOL, HAYES

In late July 1919 a war memorial to the fallen was presented to Dr. Triplett's School. It was in the form of two ebonised frames. One contained a roll of honour consisting of the names of the 41 former scholars who made the supreme sacrifice and the other showed portraits of some of them. Both were to remain permanently in the school. The school, originally in Church Walk, was demolished in 1969 and a new site found in Hemmen Lane. The whereabouts of the roll of honour and the frame of portraits are unknown, presumably lost when the old school was demolished.

HARLINGTON WAR MEMORIALS

ST. PETER and ST. PAUL'S CHURCH, ST. PETER'S WAY, HARLINGTON

In 1919 a committee was appointed for the purpose of raising funds for the erection of a memorial to the fallen in the parish Churchyard. By the end of March of that year, a substantial sum had been raised. The Right Rev. Bishop Taylor-Smith, D.D., C.V.O., Chaplain-General to the Forces conducted the ceremony. The memorial stands in the old cemetery, under the shade of the famous old yew tree which had stood for over 800 years. It is a beautiful simple Celtic cross of Cornish grey granite and stands on a raised mound overlooking the main road.

The unveiling of the war memorial at Harlington (Hillingdon Local Studies, Archives and Museum Service)

It records the names of the 75 men of the parish who were killed in action or died of wounds. Their names are inscribed in plain, black letters beneath a simple inscription which reads: 'To the Glory of God, this monument is erected in proud and loving memory of the men from this parish who fell in the Great War, 1914-1919'. It was unveiled in August 1921 in part of the old Churchyard where it can be seen. There was already a simple memorial tablet in the parish church, containing 60 names, which was unveiled in mid 1919, which replaced a temporary Roll of Honour hanging in the Church.

Forty-four further names were added after the end of the Second World War and one casualty from the Korean War is also commemorated on the memorial.

An extension of Harlington, Harmondsworth and Cranford Cottage Hospital was dedicated to the men of Harlington who laid down their lives in the Great War 1914-1919. It took the form of a new wing, consisting of an operating theatre, sterilizing room and matron's room. The building was of brick, with stone facings and a red tiled roof, in harmony with the main part of the hospital.

HARLINGTON BAPTIST CHURCH

The unveiling and dedicating of the Baptist Church memorial stained glass window on the south side of the church took place at 3pm on a Sunday afternoon in late November 1920. It was unveiled and dedicated by Col. The Rev. Sidney Jones, MC, Chaplain, RAF. No names were recorded on the two panes of the tablet as no member of the church and no man who had been in active fellowship with them had fallen in the war. However, some 'loosely' connected with the church – those who passed through the Sunday School had not returned. The memorial was dedicated as a grateful recognition of the services of those who were still alive and on a tablet below was inscribed: 'This window is dedicated to the glory of God, and in loving memory of the men from this church who laid down their lives in the Great War, 1914-1919'.

The half-circular glass at the top of the window bore a crown; the left pane, the figure of St. George and the word 'Courage'; and the right pane the Angel of Peace and the word 'Victory'.

INDEX of NAMES

Ansell	147
Beckerwick. Moses	131
Betts, Thomas	95
Beaumont, L.G.	147
Bosher, Thomas George	57
Brower, Charles	57
Butler, F.C.	132
Butler, Frank	130
Chapin, D.	131
Clark, Mr.	131
Clements, W. Leonard	147
Clucas, Private	95
Cooper, George	131
Craig, Mrs.	144
Davidson, Dr.	24
Deamer, H.	147
Donnelly, Mr.	116
Dowman, George	24
Down, John Aubrey	23
Drenon, Juan	119
Ellis, Israel	10

Erembard, Israel	153
Everall	154
Fairall, Lieutenant	148
Fairey,	36-39
Francis, Dr.	24
Gardner	106
Garrett, G.	131
Gordon, Margaret	58
Gunton, R.W.	26
Hankins, F.	129
Harvey, C.M.	93
Heyward, Mr.	119
Howard, Robert	130
Hunter, Dr.	20
Hyde	155
Hyman	131
James, Percy	27
Latham, Olive	55
Laws, Henry	138
Lethbridge, A.P.	53
Lock, Dr.	24, 144
Marchant, Mabel	55

Mellett, Herbert	67
Miller, B.J.	130
Mott, Stanley	68
Muller, Frederick	150
Muspratt, Dr.	144
Neilson, James	116
Newman, J.	91
Newton, Violet	58
Nye, J.	31
Oberfahren, Robert	151
Odell, J.	8
Ogden, P.C.	24
Paine, Roland B.	58
Pashon, Bridget	56
Perry, Annie	55
Phillips, Frank	66
Pickering, Alfred	130
Pickering, Cecil	130
Pickering, Dorothy	130
Pickering, Robert	130
Potter, Frank	67

Reid, Alfred	120
Roake, Charles	57
Roberts, Mrs.	92, 118
Robinson, William Leefe	112, 113, 138
Rodda, Raymond	129
Roseman, Myer	131
Salter, George	87
Sandow, Eugene	33, 150-151
Sargood, William	68
Shackle, Frank	28
Shadwell	68
Silverstein, Harry Meyer	145
Smith	131
Spooner, Joseph	137
Stonestreet, W.	147
Walker, Dr.	24
Watts, Charles	147, 148
Wheeler, E.	68
Zander, Scharl	153

SELECT BIBLIOGRAPHY

BENNETT, L.G. The horticultural industry of Middlesex. University of Reading, 1952

BINGHAM, S. Ministering angels. Osprey, 1979

BISHOP, W. A. The courage of the early morning. Bookprint Limited, 1966

BOURNE, J. Britain and the Great War 1914-1918. Edward Arnold, 1994

Capital Cities at War: Paris, London, Berlin, 1914-1919, edited by Jay Winter and Jean-Louis Robert. Cambridge, 1999

COLE, C. The air defence of Britain 1914-1918. Putman, 1984

COLE, G.D.H. Workshop Organisation. Oxford (Clarendon Press), 1923

DONNE, M. Per Ardua ad Astra. Frederick Muller, 1982

EVERETT, S. World War I. Bison Books, 1985

FRAZER, W.M. A History of English Public Health 1834-1939. Bailliere Tindall and Cox, 1950

GILLMAN, P. Collar the lot! How Britain interned and expelled its wartime refugees. Quartet Books, 1980

The Great War: the standard history of the all-Europe conflict, edited by H.W. Wilson. The Amalgamated Press Limited, various volumes 1916-1921

HALLEY, J.J. Squadrons of the Royal Air Force. Air-Britain, 1980

HALPENNY, B. B. Action Stations 8: Military airfields of Greater London. Patrick Stephens, 1984

HAMILTON, J.A.B. Britain's railways in World War I. George Allen and Unwin, 1967

Hayes MOH Reports 1914-1918

Hayes UDC Council Minutes 1914-1918

HUGHES, J. London since 1912. HMSO., 1973

Imperial Britain: an illustrated descriptive record of industrial achievement during the War for Freedom 1914-1918, volume I – Industrial. The St. James's Press, 1920

JACKSON, A.A. London's local railways. David and Charles, 1978

JEFFORD, C.G. Observers and Navigators and other non-pilot aircrew in the RFC, RNAS and RAF. Airlife, 2001

KELTER, C. Hayes Past. Historical Publications, 1996

KING, P. Women rule the plot: the story of the 100 year fight to establish women's place in farm and garden. Duckworth, 1999

L'encyclopedie illustre de l'aviation. Editions Atlas, 1985

LETHBRIDGE, M. Fortune Grass. Geoffrey Bles,

LEWIS, P. Squadron histories, RFC, RNAS and RAF., 1912-59. Putnam, 1959

LIDDLE, P. The airman's war. Blandford Press, 1987

LYSONS, D. An historical account of those parishes in the County of Middlesex which are described in the environs of London. 1800

MACDERMOT, E.T. History of the Great Western Railway, volume II 1863-1921. GWR Co., 1931

McMILLAN, J. The way it was 1914-1934. William Kimber and Co. Ltd., 1979

MARSHALL, J. The history of the Great West Road. Hounslow Leisure Services, 1995

MORRIS, J. The German air raids on Great Britain 1914-1918. H. Pordes, 1969

NORRIS, G. The Royal Flying Corps: a history. Frederick Muller, 1965

The official history of the Ministry of Munitions, volumes X and X11: the supply of munitions. Naval and Military Press/The Imperial War Museum, 2008

PARISH, H.J. A history of immunization. E. and S. Livingstone, 1965

PEARCE, K.R. Lowe and Shawyer Nursery. Handwritten, 1972

PHEBY, C.E. Providence. IN The Uxbridge Record, No. 69, Autumn 1997

PLUMRIDGE, J.H. Hospital ships and ambulance trains. Seeley, Service & Co., 1975

PRATT, E.A. British railways and the Great War. Selwyn and Blount, 1921

Prisoners of War Bureau. List of places of internment. No date

RAWLINSON, A. The defence of London, 1915-1918. Andrew Melrose, 1924

REYNOLDS, G.W. The night the police went on strike. Weidenfeld and Nicolson, 1968

ROBINSON, D.H. The Zeppelin in combat: a history of the German Naval Airship Division, 1912-1918. G.T. Foulis, 1971

Soldiers' and Sailors' Families Associations (Uxbridge Division of Middlesex) reports 1914-c1916.

Southall-Norwood Council Minutes 1914-1918

SOUTHERTON, P. The story of a prison. Osprey, 1975

TAYLOR, A.J.P. English history 1914-1945. Oxford at the Clarendon Press, 1976

The Times History of the War. The Times 1914-1919

TWINCH, C. Women on the land: their story during two world wars. Lutterworth Press, 1990

Victorian Harlington. The Hayes and Harlington Local History Society, 1985

WILLIAMS, J. The home fronts: Britain, France and Germany 1914-1918. Constable, 1972

WILSON, T. The Myriad faces of war: Britain and the Great War 1914-1918. Polity Press, 1988

WILSON, The Great War. Amalgamated Press, 1920s

WINTER, J.M. The Great War and the British People. Palgrave Macmillan, 2003.